Guide To Downtown Toronto Condo Prices

An Expert Guide To Your Favourite Downtown Neighbourhoods

Avoid Making An Awful Buying Decision

Instead, Ensure You Completely Understand Today's Market Before Committing!

Thomas Cook

Copyright © 2018 Thomas Cook
All rights reserved.
ISBN-10: 198748620X
ISBN-13: 978-1987486209

ARE YOU A TORONTO CONDO OR HOUSE BUYER?

If you are, you might benefit greatly from reading one or both of these books too

Get a clear understanding about everything you need to know when buying a Toronto condo or house

Free download at…

UltimateHomeBuyersGuide.com

Avoid costly mistakes when getting pre-approved for a mortgage

Free download at…

HomeBuyersFinancingGuide.com

ABOUT THE AUTHOR

Let's start off by giving you a little background about where I'm coming from in terms of experience and knowledge. I've been in the real estate industry since 1980. While originally with Royal LePage, I switched to RE/MAX Hallmark in 1983, where I have been ever since.

Along with helping literally thousands of people to buy and sell their homes, over the years I've been involved in a number of other real estate related activities as well. For example, through the '80s I had a property management company and at times managed up to 350 single-family homes, duplexes, triplexes, condos, and small four- and eight-unit buildings, mainly for investors but often for people who were out of the city on a job transfer and wanted to maintain their existing residence.

That has provided some great insight into such things as tenant related issues, understanding of the Tenant Protection Act, and knowledge on how to design a really good rental application and a comprehensive lease. I find those things help today with clients who are interested in buying something that has a rental component to it — maybe the traditional basement rental apartment where the owner lives upstairs, or more likely today a downtown Toronto condominium suite.

I've renovated about twenty-five homes in Toronto, as well as building a triplex from the ground up in Riverdale. In 2008, I built a cottage in the Kawarthas that started with an uncleared lot. These experiences certainly provided some great insights into working with contractors, dealing with City Hall for building permits, and even on occasion going to the Committee of Adjustment or the OMB (Ontario Municipal Board) when obtaining a permit requires applying for a variance.

I find these experiences help with clients who might be interested in buying something that needs renovation or fix up work. For example, a common question that both house and condo buyers ask is, "Can we take out that wall between the kitchen and the dining room? We'd like to have a more open concept there. Is that a structural wall? And if it is, how do we open it up and support it so we don't damage the integrity of the entire structure while we're doing that?"

I can certainly offer advice and answer those kinds of questions for my clients — and many more.

For several years, I also had a mortgage company, which provided a lot of insight into mortgage financing. As a result, I'm quite knowledgeable about how to package the buyer's mortgage application to get clients the best possible rate and terms along the way.

Here's How To Get In Touch...

Thomas Cook
Real Estate Sales Representative @ RE/MAX Hallmark Realty Ltd Brokerage

Mobile | 647-962-1650
Office | 416-465-7850
Email | Thomas@LivingInToronto.com

Author | Ultimate Toronto Home Buyer's Guide
Author | Toronto Home Buyer's Financing Guide
Author | Free Government Money Report
Author | Insider Tips For Getting The Best Price (condo sellers)
Author | Guide To Attracting The Best Tenants
Author | Best Capital Gains Tax Advice (investors)
Author | Insider Advice For House Sellers

Web | LivingInToronto.com

Experience || Thousands of homes sold since 1980
Professional Designations || ABR, SRES
Awards || RE/MAX's 2ND highest award - Circle Of Legends
Charity Support || Over $117,500 contributed to the Toronto Sick Kids Hospital
Speaker & Agent Coach || Delivered seminars and presentations to the public and Realtors about buying and selling real estate since 1995

THE EVOLUTION OF LIVING IN DOWNTOWN TORONTO

Not too many years ago, living in downtown Toronto wasn't all that attractive. It was a big deal to want to live in a condo 'all the way' west to King and Bathurst and there was almost zero condo development east of Yonge except south of Front Street East. Downtown streets were, for the most part, empty after dark once all the office workers had gone home.

An attractive downtown lifestyle basically did not exist for many people.

That situation started to change in a big way once two things happened. First, the Government of Ontario set Greenbelt construction restrictions on vast areas of land around the perimeter of the GTA and, at the same time, commenced with promoting intensification in existing communities to help stop the sprawl of low-rise houses.

Second, the City of Toronto changed the zoning in many downtown neighbourhoods to allow high-rise development. At first there was resistance from City planners and local Toronto communities, but many developers took their plans to the Ontario Municipal Board (OMB) and got them approved anyway.

As new condominium buildings became occupied, there began to be more people out walking Toronto's streets day and night. That brought more restaurants and other businesses.

Meanwhile, no new highways were being constructed into Toronto and travel times to work downtown from the suburban communities became longer and longer.

This evolution continued as each new condo building got constructed and another 300-700+ residents moved in.

Multiply this by 10 - 20 or more new low- and high-rise condo buildings coming on stream downtown each and every year over the past fifteen plus years and you get to what we have today… a vibrant, interesting and exciting lifestyle where many people from all walks of life want to live in the heart of Toronto where owning a car is not as necessary as it once was.

Guide To Downtown Toronto Condo Prices

As A Toronto Condo Buyer, You Have 4 Options…

Of course, when buying your Toronto condo or house, you always have four choices…

- You could decide to do nothing… after hearing what the market is doing, or finding out what your down payment situation or credit score is right now, you may make the decision to hold off purchasing for several months or longer
- You could try to buy a condo on your own without having a buyer agent represent you… every year about 5% of Toronto purchases are made by people buying on their own
- You may decide to work with one of the 50,000+ agents now registered with the Toronto Real Estate Board, many of which have very little if any experience in all the facets of home buying and properly representing their buyer client
- OR you may decide to work with a 'By Referral Only' Realtor like myself… someone whose goal is to provide such exceptional service that you'll feel compelled to refer all your friends and family for years to come

So, read on, build your knowledge and, if you feel like I've added some value to you, please feel free to contact me anytime with your questions and for help to find the perfect home for you.

Thomas Cook
Author

CONTENTS

1	Be Confident About Where To Make The Best Condo Investment	1
2	C01 Sub-Districts – Waterfront Harbourfront West, CityPlace, Entertainment District	3
3	C01 Sub-Districts – Niagara King West, Queen West, Liberty Village, Fort York	16
4	C01 Sub-Districts – Bay Street Corridor	28
5	C01 Sub-Districts – Trinity Bellwoods	34
6	C01 Sub-Districts – Kensington - Chinatown	39
7	C01 Sub-Districts – Little Portugal	44
8	C08 Sub-Districts – Waterfront Communities Distillery District, Canary District, River City, St Lawrence Market, Harbourfront East	49
9	C08 Sub-Districts – Church-Yonge Corridor	64
10	C08 Sub-Districts – Moss Park	69
11	C08 Sub-Districts – Regent Park	74
12	C02 Sub-Districts – The Annex - Yorkville	80
	A Final Summary…	85
	2018 Downtown Condo Market Projections	88
	Here's The Free Stuff You Can Get From Us	89

CHAPTER 1
BE CONFIDENT ABOUT WHERE TO MAKE THE BEST CONDO INVESTMENT

This is the Guide you've been waiting for and it's been a long time coming. A lot of market and statistical research has gone into this book to make sure you, as a downtown Toronto condo buyer, have the best information available to make a smart, educated buying decision.

I've been helping Toronto buyers since 1980 and have found that there are a series of questions that almost every purchaser asks, or at least thinks.

People always want to know…
- what's the best neighbourhood for their lifestyle
- what's public transit like in a neighbourhood and where can they easily access major highways
- are some neighbourhoods safer than others
- which areas are more affordable than others
- where are there more available condo suites in the size and price range that's affordable for them
- of all the downtown districts, which have the best appreciation
- I'm interested in a higher-end suite… where is the best selection
- and, if you're an investor, where are the best places to buy to get the ideal tenant paying an acceptable rent

This Guide will attempt to answer most of your 'big picture' questions but keep in mind that, when buying real estate, there's almost always some compromise required.

For condominium suites, compromises need to be made most typically between location, price and suite size.

Many of our clients have had constraints or requirements with at least one of those variables but that's OK. Our job as your real estate advisor is to help you navigate through the process with the least stress and most excitement at the conclusion of your condo search.

Neighbourhoods To Choose From

This is where it all starts. Buyers most often have some specific ideas about where downtown they'd like to live or purchase. In the last 15 years downtown Toronto has had a rapid expansion.

The Toronto Real Estate Board (TREB) has divided downtown first of all between east of Yonge and west of Yonge from the lake north typically to Bloor Street and, within those geographic boundaries, into what they call sub-districts. Then the community itself has named several neighbourhoods within some of those TREB sub-districts.

Many of these neighbourhoods have become well known such as Harbourfront, CityPlace, the Entertainment District, King West, Distillery and more.

In this Guide, I've broken down TREB sub-districts into their distinct neighbourhoods where they colloquially exist or stuck to the somewhat arbitrarily named TREB sub-districts where there are no mini-neighbourhoods associated with them.

I'll start with the sub-districts and neighbourhoods of the TREB C01 district which encompasses condo suites west of Yonge and south of Bloor.

Next you can read about the sub-districts and neighbourhoods of the TREB C08 district which stretches east from Yonge over to the Don River and north to Bloor.

I've taken some 'liberties' when colloquial neighbourhood names do not line up perfectly with the Toronto Real Estate Board district/sub-district boundaries. I've chosen to go with the more commonly known 'street definitions' of neighbourhoods.

No downtown summary would be complete without talking about the luxury market around Yorkville as well which is situated in the TREB C02 district.

I hope that these summaries will make it easier for you to compare downtown Toronto neighbourhoods and help you decide which works best for you.

CHAPTER 2
C01 SUB-DISTRICTS
WATERFRONT COMMUNITIES…
HARBOURFRONT WEST, CITYPLACE, ENTERTAINMENT DISTRICT

C01 Waterfront Communities

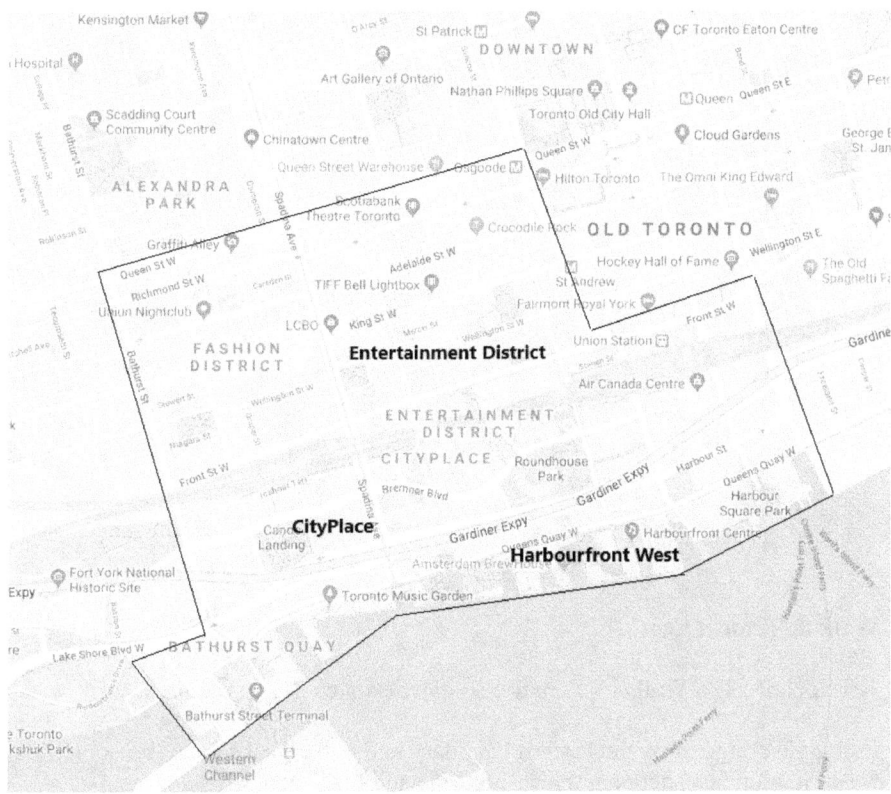

The C01 Waterfront Communities is comprised of three of the most well-known and popular neighbourhoods in downtown Toronto – Harbourfront West, CityPlace and the Entertainment District.

Let's discuss these one by one.

Harbourfront WEST

Area Boundaries & Housing Mix

The Harbourfront West neighbourhood consists of a mix of low and high-rise condominium residences, some rentals and some office towers making it a very lively area 7 days a week.

The Harbourfront West neighbourhood stretches along the Toronto waterfront from Yonge Street west to Stadium road and north to Lakeshore Blvd West. It also includes a little jog north on Lower Simcoe St and then east on Bremner Blvd to the Air Canada Centre.

Walk & Transit Score

This location is a Walker's Paradise so daily errands do not require a car.

Using 10 Yonge St on the eastern boundary and 650 Queens Quay West on the western boundary, here are their walk, ride and bike scores…

Guide To Downtown Toronto Condo Prices

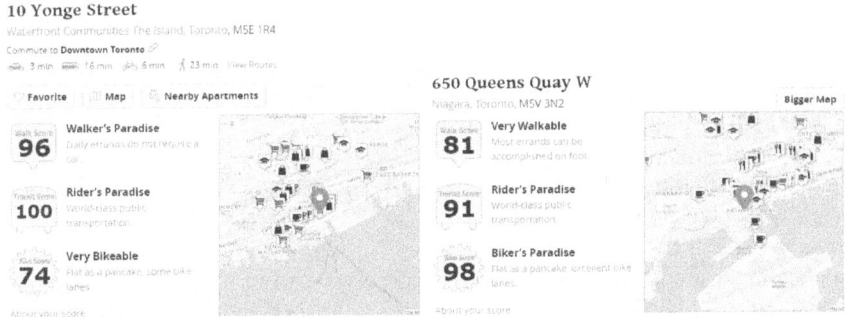

Best LOCAL Features

Shopping and Entertainment

There's certainly lots to do and experience along Toronto's prime waterfront neighbourhood.

The Harbourfront Centre is located at 235 Queens Quay W just west of Lower Simcoe St. They work with over 400 different community organizations as a lakeside cultural hub with dance, modern art, craft & theatre spaces. This lakeside venue hosts close to 4,000 events per year, including workshops, festivals and food fairs. There are also many theatrical events, artists in residence and art exhibits open to the public. In winter the Natrel Rink has "learn to skate" lessons, recreational skate and parties.

The Queens Quay Terminal just west of York St is open seven days a week and features two floors of shops, and offers a Sobey's grocery store plus several high-end shops, galleries, and restaurants.

Numerous other restaurants are located all along both the north and south sides of Queens Quay.

The relatively new separated-from-traffic bicycle trail stretches all along both Queens Quay East and West and connects to the Martin Goodman trail at both ends.

Harbourfront is conveniently located within walking distance of the St. Lawrence Market, Toronto's oldest and largest food market.

A giant Loblaws food and retail centre is located on Queens Quay East at the foot of Jarvis Street although at some point in the next few years that location will disappear due to a new condo building going up. A replacement is being built right now at the NW corner of Bathurst and Lakeshore West.

Transportation

Queens Quay has a dedicated streetcar line, along with dedicated car lanes and bicycle lanes. The streetcar runs all along Queen's Quay, from Bay to Bathurst, connecting to city bus and subway routes.

Take the ferry to the Toronto Islands from the Jack Layton Ferry Terminal at 9 Queens Quay West.

Few neighbourhoods in the world are as short a waterfront walk from an airport – the island Billy Bishop Airport is conveniently located right next door at the foot of Bathurst Street south of Queens Quay. The Billy Bishop Airport is the home of Porter Airlines and is also served by an Air Canada subsidiary.

The Gardiner Expressway / Lake Shore Boulevard, and the Don Valley Parkway are all close by for drivers to access areas east, west, north, and beyond the city.

Parks

Multiple parks are located all along Queens Quay West with two more in the planning stages.

The HTO Park and HTO Park West are close to Spadina Avenue as are the Spadina Quay Wetlands and the Toronto Music Garden. Then there's Harbour Square Park, Ann Tindal Park, Rees Street Park, Ireland Park, Little Norway Park, Stadium Road Park, and the Waterfront Trail too.

Don't forget… take a short ferry ride to the Toronto Islands and you've got a walking, biking, relaxing paradise.

Boating and Other Recreation

You can rent canoes, kayaks and small power boats at the Harbourfront Canoe & Kayak Centre located at 283 Queens Quay W. If you're a boat owner, there are very occasionally boat slips available for rent along the shoreline.

More Neighbourhood Features

There's a City School for kindergarten through grade 8 at the SE corner of Bathurst.

Who Might Love Living Here And Why

Almost anyone… young couples, retirees, singles and families with small children would enjoy living close to the lake

There is an almost endless supply of things to do, and the amenities are good – shopping, dining, etc. And the downtown hub is just a few minutes north of here. Harbourfront is definitely one of Toronto's most sought-after neighbourhoods to live and play in.

Downside To Living Here

There's a downside? Possibly the summer crowds out walking or biking and enjoying the fresh air and sunshine. And it's a little 'fresh' with the wind in the middle of the winter but we're Canadians right?

What's The Real Estate Market Like Here

The downtown condo market is busy overall, but demand is high for suites in Harbourfront West.

CityPlace

Area Boundaries & Housing Mix

CityPlace is bordered by Lake Shore Boulevard on the south and goes north to Front St West and from Bathurst Street east to the Rogers Centre.

This community didn't exist before 2002 when the first 4 buildings were constructed along the south side of Front just east of Spadina. Now there are just a few condo building lots left close to Bathurst which are still open for development.

There is no shortage of beautiful condos to choose from at CityPlace, each with a variety of styles, finishes and amenities. Buyers are sure to find what they're looking for here, in a prime location in the City of Toronto.

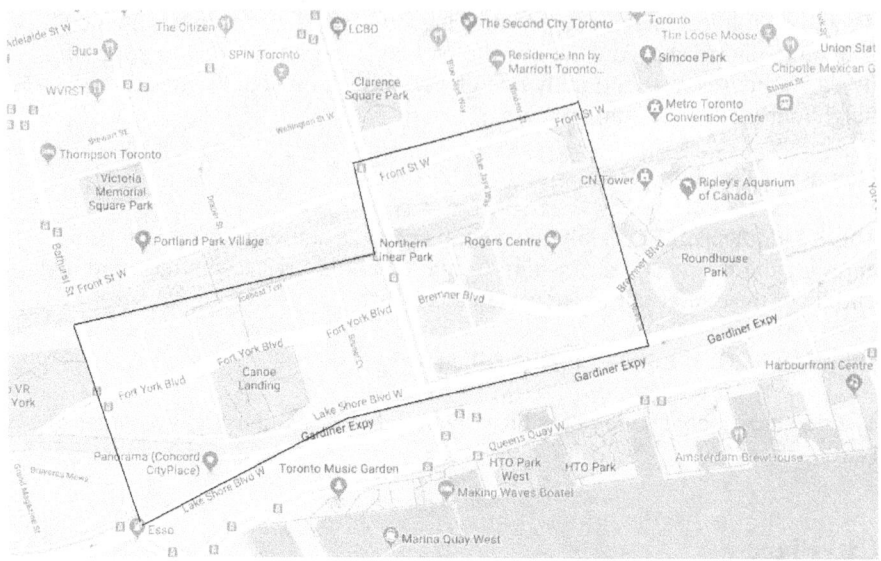

Walk & Transit Score

Using 361 Front St W at the Northeast corner... and 38 Dan Leckie Way at the southwest corner...

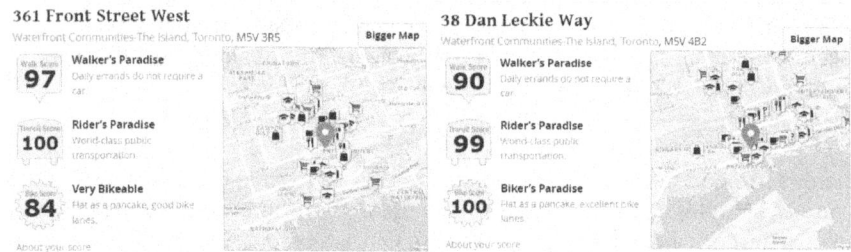

Best LOCAL Features

Shopping and Entertainment

CityPlace residents have countless options close by. The Entertainment district, the Fashion District, Kensington Market, Chinatown and the Toronto Waterfront are all within walking distance. In addition, the C.N. Tower, the Harbourfront Antique Market, the Canadian National Exhibition grounds, the Fort York historical park, the Marine Museum, Old Fort York, Ripley's Aquarium of Canada and the Metro Toronto Convention Centre are all adjacent to, or nearby this neighbourhood.

Along Fort York Boulevard there are several pubs and a Sobey's Urban Fresh grocery store along with a City of Toronto library.

Also, CityPlace residents can enjoy a variety of sport and entertainment events year-round at the nearby Air Canada Centre and Rogers Centre. Roy Thompson Hall and the TIFF Bell Lightbox are close by on King. There are numerous trendy shops and restaurants along King Street West and Queen Street West and in nearby Liberty Village.

Transportation

There is a north-south streetcar on Spadina Ave, right in the centre of CityPlace which can take you south to the lake or north to either the King or Queen east-west streetcar lines. There is relatively easy access to Union Station which includes subway, railway and commuter bus service. At the western end of CityPlace, there's also a north-south streetcar along Bathurst.

The Gardiner Expressway / Lake Shore Boulevard, and DVP are all close by for drivers to access areas east, west, north, and beyond the city.

You can take the ferry to the Toronto Islands from Jack Layton Ferry Terminal at 9 Queens Quay W.

The Toronto island Billy Bishop Airport is conveniently located very close by at the foot of Bathurst Street south of Queens Quay.

Parks

The Canoe Landing park spans 8 acres and is the largest greenspace in this neighbourhood and the social hub of the area. It is a park designed in partnership with famous Canadian artist and author Douglas Coupland that also serves as home to several of his sculptures. There are numerous neighbourhood events that take place in Canoe Landing Park.

Roundhouse Park, just east of here is part of the railway museum, and offers restored train equipment & miniature stream train rides.

Since the waterfront is nearby, you can also enjoy the HTO Park and HTO Park West which are close to Spadina Avenue as are the Spadina Quay Wetlands and the Toronto Music Garden. Rees Street Park and the Waterfront Trail are also in or near this area. At the western end, there's easy access to the historical Fort York park.

Don't forget… take a short ferry ride to the Toronto Islands and you've got a walking, biking, relaxing paradise.

More Neighbourhood Features

The Financial District is a short walk or bike ride and there is a string of hospitals on University Ave from Dundas to College.

Who Might Love Living Here And Why

CityPlace is a trendy urban playground that is the ideal place to live for both young professionals and young families - Professional singles and couples who choose to live downtown and enjoy a commute-free life, with a work and play lifestyle will love the carefree life in CityPlace.

Young families also call CityPlace home, due to family-friendly accommodations being answered by buildings currently in development that include schools and daycares. Empty nesters enjoy life here too, as there is an almost endless supply of things to do. And if you travel, you can lock up and go.

Downside To Living Here

I can't think of any, except you could join in with the revelers after an event at Rogers Centre or ACC.

What's The Real Estate Market Like Here

Very busy… the location almost in the middle of downtown Toronto makes it attractive to many buyers and renters.

Entertainment District

Area Boundaries & Housing Mix

The general boundaries of the Entertainment District are from Front St W north to Queen West and from Bathurst St east to University Ave.

Sitting comfortably between the Fashion District to the west and the Financial District to the east, the trendy Queen West neighbourhood is on the north border of this neighbourhood and CityPlace and Harbourfront are to the south.

Since 2000, the area has seen a big condo construction boom and several of the remaining historic warehouses and factories have been converted into lofts.

Whether you are planning on living in Toronto's Entertainment District or want to invest in a condo, the Entertainment District offers everything from newer condos to loft conversions to combination "condotels" – condos with boutique hotel amenities and service.

Guide To Downtown Toronto Condo Prices

Walk & Transit Score

Using The Peter Street Condos at 101 Peter Street, roughly in the middle

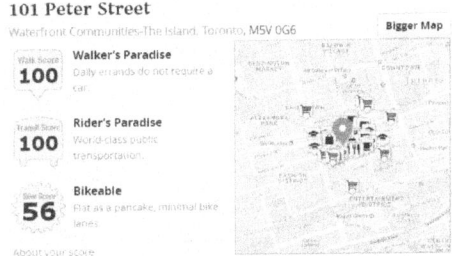

Best LOCAL Features

Shopping and Entertainment

Formerly the very industrial Garment District, fashion and textile manufacturing began to leave their large warehouses and factories behind as they moved away from the District in the 1970s.

In the 1980s nightclubs began to move into these vacant spaces. A decade later, the Toronto Entertainment District was actually one of the biggest nightclub hotspots in North America, along with being home to many restaurants and bars.

The Entertainment District hosts The Toronto International Film Festival at the TIFF Bell Lightbox, among other venues. It is also home to many performing arts centres, family attractions, theatres and close to the Rogers Centre for concerts and the city's biggest sports teams.

Transportation

Close to transit, immensely walkable and always bustling with fine dining, nightlife, festivals and entertainment, the aptly-named Entertainment District is a great place to live. Streetcars run east-west along King and Queen with a north-south streetcar on Spadina. Union Station and the University subway line all serve this neighbourhood. The Gardiner Expressway / Lakeshore Blvd are to the south, and Billy Bishop airport is close by.

Parks

Clarence Square Park on Spadina Avenue just north of Front Street features a mature tree canopy, many park benches and an enclosed dog off-leash area. It is a relatively quiet and shady park, with a spacious grassy terrain. Simcoe Park is a small parkette across the street from the Toronto Convention Centre and is a good spot to eat lunch or have a quiet moment.

More Neighbourhood Features

The Ripley's Aquarium and the Toronto Convention Centre are also located near here.

The Financial District is close by and there is a string of hospitals on University Ave from Dundas to College.

Who Might Love Living Here And Why

Professional singles and couples who choose to live downtown and enjoy a commute free life, with a work and play lifestyle. Artists, musicians and creative tech types enjoy the colourful and eclectic mix of venues and shops here. Empty nesters enjoy life here too, as there is an almost endless supply of nice restaurants and theatres.

Downside To Living Here

It gets a little busy on the weekends with the sidewalks crowded with people out enjoying Toronto's nightlife. If you don't like crowds and people enjoying the terrific entertainment venues that Toronto has to offer, you'll want to look elsewhere.

What's The Real Estate Market Like Here

The downtown condo market has been booming with new construction for over 15 years now and it's matured very nicely. With the advent of the Ontario Government's intensification initiatives and the cost of semi- and detached homes rising considerably, purchasing a downtown condo for both affordability and exciting lifestyle has become very attractive.

Despite new investment rules and mortgage qualification restrictions, the downtown condo market has remained very busy with 'above-average' appreciation annually over the recent past.

2017 SOLD Statistics For C01 Waterfront-West

Suite Sales Numbers By Unit Size

2017 Units By Size	C01 - Waterfront	% Of market
# of bachelor units SOLD	99	4%
# of 1-and 1+den SOLD	1833	65%
# of 2-bedrooms SOLD	807	29%
# of 3-bedrooms SOLD	81	3%
TOTAL UNIT SALES=>	2820	

Suite Sales #'s Score = 5

What Kind Of Inventory Is There?

2017 Sales by PRICE Range	C01 - Waterfront	% Of market
$300-399K	240	9%
$400-499K	828	29%
$500-599K	703	25%
$600-699K	421	15%
$700-799K	229	8%
$800-899K	162	6%
$900-999K	71	3%
$1M – 1.5M	104	4%
$1.5M PLUS	63	2%
Total Sales Between $400,000 and $600,000 = 54%		

Affordability - Average Sale Price (Scored on a 1-5 scale, 5 being highest)

	C01 - Waterfront
Running Average Sale Price	$636,274

Affordability Score = 4

Best Appreciation (Scored on a 1-5 scale, 5 being highest)

	C01 - Waterfront
Average Y-O-Y Sale Price Change From 2016	27%

Appreciation Score = 4

Best Investment Conclusion (Scored on a 1-5 scale, 5 being highest)

My investment conclusion is based on sales numbers, average purchase price, appreciation history, location downtown and rental potential in each TREB sub-district.

C01 Waterfront in 2017 had the highest number of sales of all the C01 sub-districts (means liquidity is easily available if you need it), the second highest year-over-year appreciation and the second highest number of condo suites selling between $400,000 and $600,000.

Investment Score = 5

CHAPTER 3
C01 SUB-DISTRICTS
NIAGARA...
KING WEST, QUEEN WEST, LIBERTY VILLAGE, FORT YORK

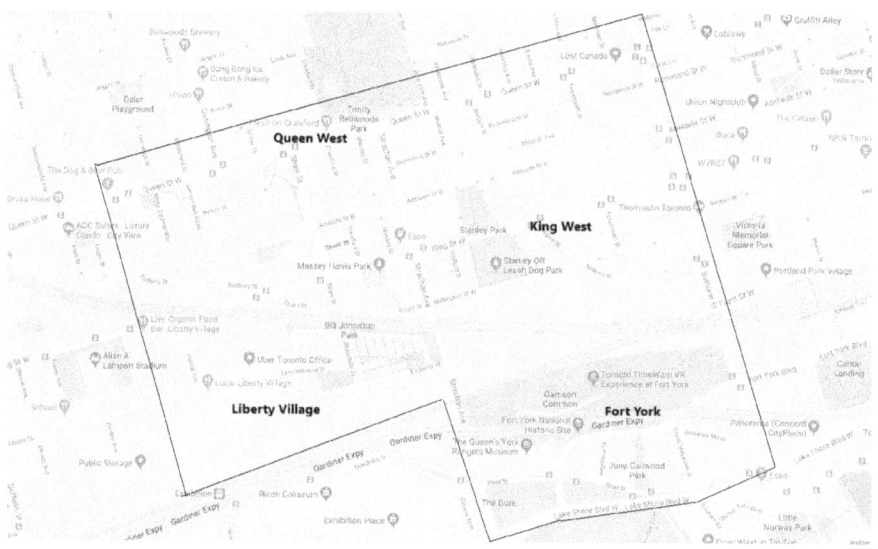

The Niagara TREB sub-district is comprised of four very popular neighbourhoods including King West and Queen West, Liberty Village and Fort York.

King West & Queen West

Area Boundaries & Housing Mix

For purposes of this analysis, the King / Queen West neighbourhoods include from Bathurst west to Sudbury St / Gladstone and from Front Street West north to just above Queen West. It tends to follow along the north side of the railway tracks as they bend north just west of Strachan Ave.

Guide To Downtown Toronto Condo Prices

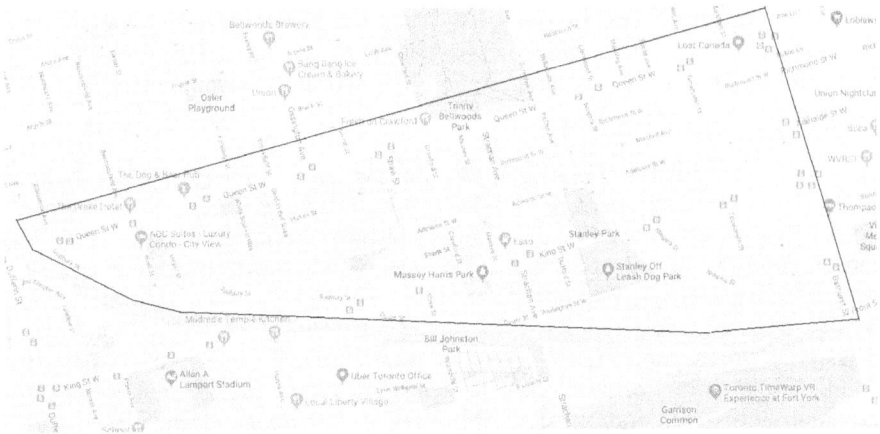

In the 1990s, most of the industrial and manufacturing businesses left their factories behind when they moved out of the area, which were then converted into authentic and spacious loft-style condos and revitalized loft office space. King / Queen West is the ultimate in life/work balance with a number of these converted hard loft spaces that can double as workspaces as well as many larger, more recently-built condo towers.

Walk & Transit Score

Using 800 King St West and 48 Abell Street close to Queen West

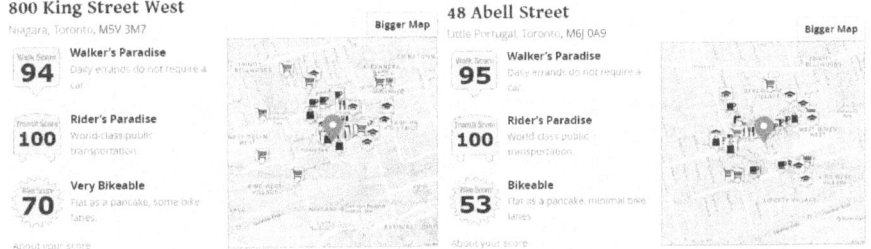

Best LOCAL Features

Shopping and Entertainment

The stylish King West neighbourhood in downtown Toronto is well-known for being home to the next big thing in hot, high-end restaurants, trendy shops, bars, dance clubs and lounges.

While the vibrant neighbourhood itself offers plenty in terms of nightlife and things to do, it's also within walking distance to Chinatown, the Theatre District (including Canada's Walk of Fame, Roy Thomson Hall and the Toronto International Film Festival) and the Financial District. So, whatever you find yourself up to in this busy neighbourhood, you'll be able to walk home afterwards.

Next to the theatre district and close to Chinatown and Kensington Market, the Queen West area has grown into a hub for the arts and is home to a number of notable tourist attractions like the Gladstone Hotel, Trinity Bellwoods Park, the Drake, Graffiti Alley and of course, 299 Queen Street West, the former MuchMusic and City TV building.

The Westernmost part of Queen West, or West Queen West, is known as the Art and Design district. This is an upscale, gentrified and trendy area that is home to boutique stores, restaurants, cafes, fabric shops, clothing stores and plenty of live entertainment.

The Drake and Gladstone hotels along Queen West have been renovated and now provide upscale entertainment venues. Ossington Avenue just north of Queen has become a go-to spot for dining along with several low-rise condo residences.

Transportation

It's also easy to get around, as the neighbourhood is perfect for pedestrians and transit users with easy access to the 501 Streetcar, which travels along Queen Street every 6 minutes.

Parks

There are quite a few parks and greenspaces in this area. Starting at the Bathurst side… Stanley Park runs north and south of King between Stanley Terrace, just east of Strachan, and Walnut Ave. A large part of the park on the south side is devoted to the Stanley Off Leash Dog Park.

Massey Harris Park is a small park at King and Crawford. Trinity-Bellwoods is a very large park north of Queen and east of Crawford, with a farmer's market In the summer and lots of other amenities. Other small parks in the are on the western side are Joseph Workman, Paul Garfinkel Parkette and Osler Playground.

More Neighbourhood Features

Queen West also has its own Business Improvement Area, representing over 300 business owners and merchants who work hard to keep the neighbourhood a thriving destination.

Who Might Love Living Here And Why

Whether you're a first-time condo buyer, an investor or are looking to move closer to the hustle and bustle of downtown, you're sure to be happy making your home here.

King / Queen West is home to young, urban professionals, and most of the commercial spaces here have a contemporary New York-feel as they're home to advertising, design or high-tech technology companies. The area is also highly walkable and served by both streetcar and subway lines, and since almost everything you need is at your fingertips, a car is not needed.

Downside To Living Here

On a weekend night, there's lots of traffic along both King and Queen with locals out for a good time with their friends.

It's a little further from the "downtown" hub but, on the plus side, it's also west of the downtown traffic if you want to travel to the western parts of the GTA.

What's The Real Estate Market Like Here

Prices are a little lower as you get towards King and Queen West including some off of Sudbury Street.

Both neighbourhoods are very popular for live-in owners and investors.

Liberty Village

Area Boundaries & Housing Mix

The boundaries for Liberty Village are the railway tracks on the north (just south of King) and south to the Gardiner Expressway and from Strachan Avenue in the east to Dufferin Street in the west. It's situated right between the Parkdale and Fort York neighbourhoods.

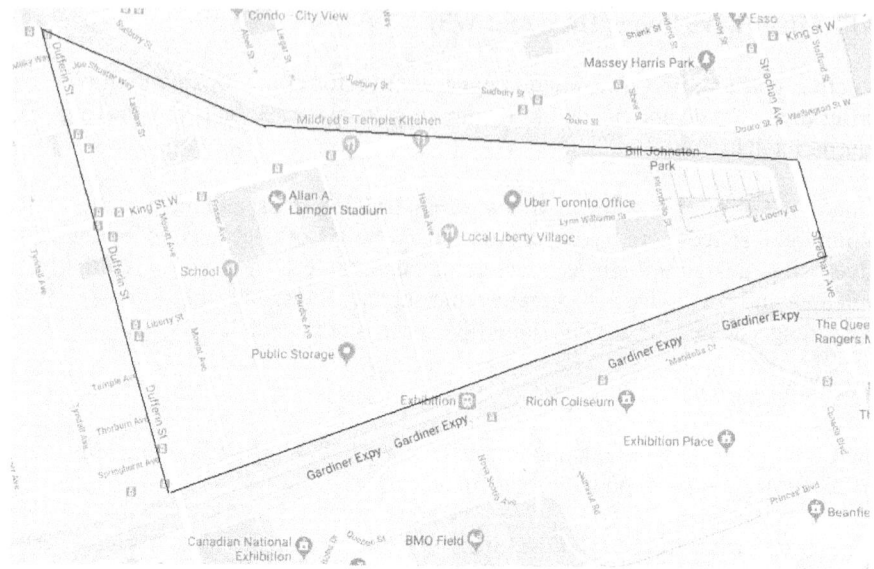

Liberty Village is one of Toronto's oldest downtown neighbourhoods. The name Liberty comes from Liberty Street, the street on which prisoners first walked free from the Toronto Central Prison starting in the 1870's.

Starting in 2004 with the beginning of new condo construction, Liberty Village has become a hot residential area. A number of gorgeous authentic industrial buildings have been updated and converted into either loft condo apartments or high-tech business offices.

Many new high-rise condos and low-rise stacked townhouses have been built in the last 12-15 years and the neighbourhood is almost built-out now.

Walk & Transit Score

Using a fairly central location of the King West Condos at 65 East Liberty St

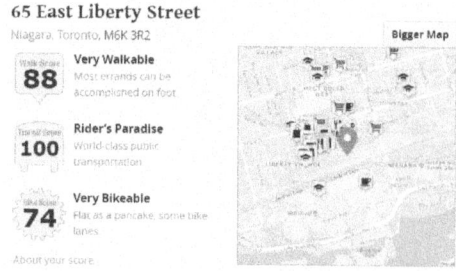

Best LOCAL Features

This historical neighbourhood has gone through many different transitional periods to become the residential hotspot and great place to live and work that it is today.

Shopping and Entertainment

There are offices here, as well as a number of hot restaurants, shops, gyms, a big Metro grocery store and art galleries. The office spaces tend to be concentrated in the west end over to Dufferin while condos are situated east of Hanna Avenue.

Life in Liberty Village means also means being nearby farmers markets, patios, and food and drink festivals.

Local Liberty Village is a relaxed neighbourhood hangout with rotating taps of craft beer, modern bar food & sports on TV. School is a chic eatery with industrial decor & two patios, serving brunch, lunch & dinner, and drinks. Live Organic Food Bar -Liberty Village is a plant-based, organic, gluten and refined sugar-free restaurant.

Allan A. Lamport Stadium, is a multi-purpose stadium on King Street West in Liberty Village, currently serving as the home field of the Toronto Wolfpack, Toronto FC II and the Canada national rugby league team. Ricoh Coliseum is another sports venue on Manitoba Dr.

Just southwest of here is Medieval Times Dinner & Tournament, a fun place to take visitors, for jousting, horsemanship & falconry plus a 4-course, utensil-free meal served in a castle-like space.

Joe Rockhead's Indoor Rock Climbing is a lofty warehouse space right in this neighbourhood, with climbing walls of varying difficulty, plus bouldering & classes.

The Argonaut Rowing Club can be found on Lakeshore Blvd in Marilyn Bell Park.

Transportation

This area is served well by the King St streetcar and transit north-south on Dufferin St.

The Gardiner / Lakeshore Blvd is easily accessed from this location.

Parks

Starting in the east, there is Gateway Park, Bill Johnston park and Liberty Village Park.

Over to the northwest of this area you find Alan A Lamport Stadium is surrounded by greenspace and Dufferin-King Parkette. And of course, to the south there are the CNE grounds with Bandshell Park and Rose Garden, the Toronto Inukshuk Park, and The Gore. And southwest you find Marilyn Bell Park along the lake.

More Neighbourhood Features

There are offices here, as well as a number of hot restaurants, shops, gyms, a big Metro grocery store and art galleries. The office spaces tend to be concentrated in the west end over to Dufferin while condos are situated east of Hanna Avenue.

Life in Liberty Village means also means being nearby farmers markets, patios, and food and drink festivals.

Who Might Love Living Here And Why

Since 2004, Liberty Village has experienced a tremendous amount of rapid condominium growth and is now considered a trendy place to live by young professionals as well as artists, who appreciate its proximity to all things necessary downtown, like the financial district and key gallery, fashion and entertainment districts via only a short walk or streetcar ride.

Downside To Living Here

Sometimes a slow streetcar ride east on King to the downtown core although the TTC is expanding service frequency and capacity while the city has added some deterrence for drivers going east-west on King east of Bathurst to speed up streetcar service.

What's The Real Estate Market Like Here

Busy like elsewhere in downtown Toronto but it's almost built out which will mean less construction interruption going forward. As the proportion of renters drops over time, the neighbourhood will mature quite nicely.

Fort York

Area Boundaries & Housing Mix

The Fort York neighbourhood is bordered on the east by Bathurst Street and goes west to Strachan, and to the north by the CP/CN railway corridor and south to Lakeshore Boulevard. This almost-new area is all condo high-rise and low-rise suites plus the historic Fort York buildings also remain along with a visitor's centre and museum.

One of the oldest historic areas in Toronto (first plotted in 1793), it's also one of the newest neighbourhoods in the city, and one of the most sought-after destinations for condo buyers.

Named after the adjacent Fort York, a National Historic Site that is home to the largest group of War of 1812 period buildings in Canada.

Walk & Transit Score

Using the West Harbour City condos at 628 Fleet Street on the south side of the area

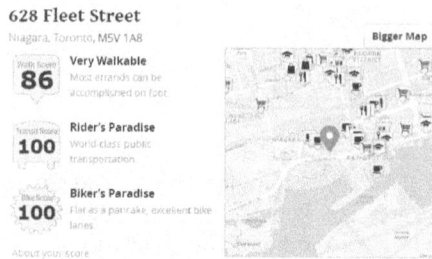

Best LOCAL Features

Shopping And Entertainment

There is plenty of shopping on King Street and along Queen's Quay West. In addition, the neighbourhood is close to the Entertainment District, Harbourfront and many others. There is entertainment, sports and home shows happening during the year at the Canadian National Exhibition (CNE) grounds. And the always entertaining waterfront, is just down the street.

Transportation

Walking, cycling and transit are all possible ways to get around in Fort York, with both Lakeshore Boulevard and the Gardiner easily accessible to drivers.

Parks

All around here are trails and parks including Coronation Park. Even closer is Garrison Common, an event space that hosts various art festivals through the year. The Fort grounds and surrounding areas also bring a welcome breath of green space into the neighbourhood, and links to the Martin Goodman Trail, a 56-kilometre trail along Lake Ontario perfect for cyclists and walking the family dog.

More Neighbourhood features

Toronto TimeWarp VR Experience at Fort York is the Story of Toronto in Virtual Reality at Fort York National Historic Site.

Who Might Love Living Here And Why

In a neighbourhood for those who want a piece of the busy city just for themselves, Fort York is very easy to get around and there's easy downtown streetcar access plus highway access going west along the Gardiner Expressway.

Downside To Living Here

Traffic is heavy for three weeks at the end of summer when the CNE is on or when summer marathons are running. On the plus side, you don't need to find parking when you want to enjoy the CNE and you can easily see the planes flying in the airshow from the neighbourhood, and from many of the suites.

What's The Real Estate Market Like Here

New construction is almost complete here now as all the building lots have 'grown' high-rise condos. There's a range of suite sizes but one- and one plus den suites predominate.

2017 SOLD Statistics For C01 Niagara

Suite Sales Numbers By Unit Size

2017 Units By Size	C01 - Niagara	% Of market
# of bachelor units SOLD	68	6%
# of 1-and 1+den SOLD	736	66%
# of 2-bedrooms SOLD	308	28%
# of 3-bedrooms SOLD	5	0.4%
TOTAL UNIT SALES=>	1117	

Suite Sales #'s Score = 4

What Kind Of Inventory Is There?

2017 Sales by PRICE Range	C01 - Niagara	% Of market
$300-399K	165	16%
$400-499K	347	34%
$500-599K	260	25%
$600-699K	148	14%
$700-799K	55	5%
$800-899K	26	3%
$900-999K	9	1%
$1M – 1.5M	18	2%
$1.5M PLUS	7	1%
Total Sales Between $400,000 and $600,000 = 59%		

Affordability - Average Sale Price (Scored on a 1-5 scale, 5 being highest)

	C01 - Niagara
Running Average Sale Price	$534,363

Affordability Score = 5

Best Appreciation (Scored on a 1-5 scale, 5 being highest)

	C01 - Niagara
Average Y-O-Y Sale Price Change From 2016	24%

Appreciation Score = 3

Best Investment Conclusion (Scored on a 1-5 scale, 5 being highest)

My investment conclusion is based on sales numbers, average purchase price, appreciation history, location downtown and rental potential in each TREB sub-district.

The Niagara District scored well because of its second highest Total Unit Sales and best affordability compared to the other C01 sub-districts.

Investment Score = 4

CHAPTER 4
C01 SUB-DISTRICT
BAY STREET CORRIDOR

Area Boundaries & Housing Mix

The Bay Street Corridor consists of condominium suites that run from Bloor south to Front Street and between Yonge and west to University Avenue.

Although there are pockets of detached houses and townhouses sprinkled in along some of the cross streets or laneways, the vast majority of the housing stock in this district are high rise condos ranging from mid-range up to luxury accommodations.

Walk & Transit Score

Using the Murano Condos at 38 Grenville Street as a 'mid-point' example,

Notably, the Bay Street Corridor is also the absolute most walkable neighbourhood in the city of Toronto and has a transit score of 100 thanks to close streetcar routes and subway lines, along with access to Toronto's underground pedestrian shopping network, PATH.

If you're looking for comfortable living, the hustle and bustle or downtown and plenty of things to see, eat and do, you're likely to find it – and within walking distance, too.

Best LOCAL Features

Shopping and Entertainment

Residents are close to everything they need when it comes to shopping and entertainment, with over 1,000 restaurants, bars and cafes in the Bay Street Corridor alone.

Both Dundas Square and the Eaton Centre are a really short walk away for lots of fun entertainment and excellent shopping.

The Cineplex/Varsity Cinemas are just south of Bloor and theatres along Yonge St north of Queen are a short walk away.

At Bloor and Queen's Park (Avenue Rd south of Bloor) are the Royal Ontario Museum with Sprawling natural history & world cultures galleries, plus dinosaurs in the Libeskind crystal wing, and the Gardiner Museum across the street. Besides exhibits, this ceramics museum offers classes, lectures & tours, plus a bistro & gift shop.

Yonge-Dundas Square at Yonge and Dundas is a bustling outdoor public space & live-event venue hosting concerts, movies & community events, across from the north end of the Eaton Centre.

Nathan Phillips Square is a lively public space in front of city hall hosting numerous events year-round with a busy ice rink in the winter and a popular New Years Eve celebration.

Both Luminato, an over two-week arts celebration, and Nuit Blanche, which takes place on one night, sunset to sunrise, are art and performance events that take place in many locations around the downtown core.

Transportation

This area is well served by transit. There is a bus north-south on Bay St, and streetcars running east-west along King, Queen, Dundas and College Streets. Subway stations are just a short walk away on Yonge or University at major streets. At the north end is the Bloor-Danforth subway line and easy access to the DVP. At the south end is the Lakeshore/Gardiner.

Parks

North to south...

There is some nice greenspace around Queen's Park and the University of Toronto campus locations, including Philosopher's Walk, a serene footpath through a landscaped park in the St. George campus of the U of T, just to the west of here, south of Bloor St.

The East of Bay Park is off Breadalbane St. There is McGill Parkette off McGill St and Ryerson Community Park off Gould, east of Yonge St. The Cloud Gardens with Cloud Gardens Conservatory is a unique urban oasis on the south side of Richmond between Yonge and Bay.

At the very bottom of Bay St, at the lake in Harbourfront West is Harbour Square Park, located next to the Toronto Ferry Docks. Harbour Square Park offers downtown folks a spot to sit and watch the ferries travel back and forth to the island. Have a picnic lunch or sit and wait for your friends here before you catch the ferry to the Toronto Islands.

More Neighbourhood Features

This densely populated area in the downtown core is known for being the hub of the fast-paced Toronto Financial District, but it's also only a short walk to a number of desirable downtown areas including downtown Yonge Street, Ryerson University, the University of Toronto and Toronto City Hall.

There is a string of hospitals and medical buildings along University between College and Dundas, just a short walk west.

Who Might Love Living Here And Why

A mix of young professionals and students make their homes here, looking for a vibrant and convenient neighbourhood within walking distance of work at the Financial District (King and Bay) or to school. This area is also 'hospital row' and many hospital staff and researchers choose to get a residence here.

Formerly known as "The Ward", the Bay Street Corridor is now recognized as one of the prime condo neighbourhoods in all of downtown Toronto and it's ideal for someone without their own car.

Downside To Living Here

It's not inexpensive but it sure is convenient!

What's The Real Estate Market Like Here

The Bay Street district is more upper-end than some of the other neighbourhoods with its easy access to Bloor Street West and easy access to the 'centre of Toronto's universe' which is Yonge Street.

There's lots of new construction going on, especially along Yonge north of Dundas.

2017 SOLD Statistics For C01 Bay Street

Suite Size Options

2017 Units By Size	C01 – Bay Street	% Of market
# of bachelor units SOLD	53	6%
# of 1-and 1+den SOLD	474	56%
# of 2-bedrooms SOLD	289	34%
# of 3-bedrooms SOLD	26	3%
TOTAL UNIT SALES=>	842	

Suite Sales #'s Score = 3

What Kind Of Inventory Is There?

2017 Sales by PRICE Range	C01 - Bay Street	% Of market
$300-399K	50	6%
$400-499K	136	16%
$500-599K	175	21%
$600-699K	127	15%
$700-799K	103	12%
$800-899K	88	11%
$900-999K	34	4%
$1M – 1.5M	76	9%
$1.5M PLUS	45	5%
Total Sales Between $400,000 and $600,000 = 37%		

Affordability - Average Sale Price (Scored on a 1-5 scale, 5 being highest)

	C01 - Bay Street
Running Average Sale Price	$748,324

Affordability Score = 3

Best Appreciation (Scored on a 1-5 scale, 5 being highest)

	C01 - Bay Street
Average Y-O-Y Sale Price Change From 2016	23%

Appreciation Score = 2

Best Investment Conclusion (Scored on a 1-5 scale, 5 being highest)

My investment conclusion is based on sales numbers, average purchase price, appreciation history, location downtown and rental potential in each TREB sub-district.

Remember please, I'm scoring these relative to the other TREB sub-districts in C01. If we were comparing Bay Street, and the other downtown sub-districts, to the rest of the city or to the GTA, they would be scored way higher on my Investment Score.

Because Bay Street has the lowest appreciation score and a low affordability score of the C01 sub-districts, I've rated it as follows.

Investment Score = 2

CHAPTER 5
C01 SUB-DISTRICT
TRINITY BELLWOODS

Trinity Bellwoods

Area Boundaries & Housing Mix

The Trinity-Bellwoods neighbourhood is bounded on the east by Bathurst Street and stretches west to Dovercourt. The southern boundary is Queen West and goes north to Colleges St.

Predominantly, Trinity-Bellwoods, named after the big park, is composed of semi and detached houses typical of the Victorian period of architecture found in many of Toronto's downtown neighbourhoods

New construction and loft conversions have been happening over the past several years in empty or under-utilized lots along many of the main arteries throughout the neighbourhood.

Walk & Transit Score

Using the 109Oz condo building at 109 Ossington Avenue,

Best LOCAL Features

Shopping and Entertainment

Most of Queen Street has an artsy flavour. This area along Queen Street includes galleries, antique shops and bookstores, vegetarian restaurants and natural food markets, cafes and restaurants, fashion and accessory stores.

Kensington Market, located just east of here is a long-standing, colourful market area for independent shops/cafes, plus produce, meat & fish stands.

Artscape Youngplace at 180 Shaw St is a community cultural hub in Toronto's West Queen West neighbourhood devoted to artistic creation, learning, and collaboration. It is part ideas laboratory and part creativity workshop with 75,000 square feet of space devoted to artistic inspiration, learning, growth and expression.

Ossington Avenue has a high concentration of bars and restaurants, cafes and coffee shops, art galleries and hip clothing stores, all catering to the youthful demographic in this neighbourhood. The Bellwoods Brewery on Ossington, has limited seasonal dishes & a rotating selection of experimental beer in a small brewhouse with patio. The Bang Bang Ice Cream & Bakery on Ossington has ice cream sandwiches on house-made cookies, cups, cones & to-go tubs in a white & pale-wood space.

For nighttime entertainment there is the Drake Hotel and the Gladstone Hotel on Queen West.

Sneaky Dee's – just off the north east corner is an unassuming casual bar serving Tex-Mex fare & known for its nachos, with edgy live music & DJs upstairs, late-night food and vegetarian options.

Transportation

This area is well served by transit – The Queen, Dundas and College streetcars run east-west while the Bathurst streetcar and Ossington bus run north-south.

Parks

For parks you have the Fred Hamilton Playground, and Trinity-Bellwoods Park, a spacious park, located in the centre of this neighbourhood and which spans the entire length north to south. It has many indoor and outdoor facilities including volleyball & tennis courts, an outdoor skating rink & indoor recreation centre. In the park you will also find the Trinity Bellwoods Farmers Market in the summer.

More Neighbourhood Features

The Toronto Western Hospital is located on the east side, on Bathurst St.

Who Might Love Living Here And Why

While the vast majority of residents live in houses, there are slowly but surely small, low-rise buildings being infilled along the major east-west and north-south streets.

Owners love the terrific community spirit and easy access to downtown or travelling west.

Downside To Living Here

The main streets are busy on weekends with people out for a good time.

What's The Real Estate Market Like Here

There's not much inventory available in this sub-district so choices are few.

2017 SOLD Statistics For C01 Trinity Bellwoods

Suite Size Options

2017 Units By Size	C01 – Trinity Bellwoods	% Of market
# of bachelor units SOLD	0	0%
# of 1-and 1+den SOLD	26	58%
# of 2-bedrooms SOLD	17	38%
# of 3-bedrooms SOLD	2	4%
TOTAL UNIT SALES=>	45	

Suite Sales #'s Score = 1

What Kind Of Inventory Is There?

2017 Sales by PRICE Range	C01 - Trinity Bellwoods	% Of market
$300-399K	4	9%
$400-499K	8	18%
$500-599K	6	3%
$600-699K	8	18%
$700-799K	6	13%
$800-899K	2	4%
$900-999K	2	4%
$1M – 1.5M	6	13%
$1.5M PLUS	3	7%
Total Sales Between $400,000 and $600,000 = 11%		

Affordability - Average Sale Price (Scored on a 1-5 scale, 5 being highest)

	C01 - Trinity Bellwoods
Running Average Sale Price	$460,704

Affordability Score = 2

Best Appreciation (Scored on a 1-5 scale, 5 being highest)

	C01 - Trinity Bellwoods
Average Y-O-Y Sale Price Change From 2016	23%

Appreciation Score = 5

Best Investment Conclusion (Scored on a 1-5 scale, 5 being highest)

My investment conclusion is based on sales numbers, average purchase price, appreciation history, location downtown and rental potential in each TREB sub-district.

Although this district scored highest on the Appreciation Score, that was mainly because of a low number of sales which skewed the rate higher. Because of this, and the low Affordability Score, I've scored it overall as follows…

Investment Score = 2

CHAPTER 6
C01 SUB-DISTRICT
KENSINGTON - CHINATOWN

Kensington-Chinatown

Area Boundaries & Housing Mix

This neighbourhood stretches from University west to Bathurst and from Queen West north to College Street.

At the southern end, you're right in the middle of Chinatown.

Kensington-Chinatown has a mix of small to moderate Victorian row-houses, many with decorative accents. Many offer rear laneways. Many new housing projects are being, or have been built, including townhomes, lofts and condominiums. There is also a mixed-income, mixed-use housing cooperative.

Walk & Transit Score

Using the Phoebe On Queen condos at 18 Beverley Street,

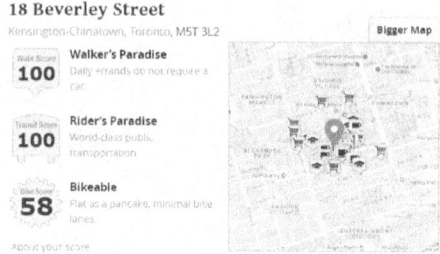

Best LOCAL Features

An eclectic, walkable, bohemian neighbourhood that draws artists and tourists, the Kensington Market area of Toronto is home to vintage shops, funky bars, food markets and ethnic restaurants. Pedestrian Sundays in the summer bring out cyclists, hippies, street performers and dogs in droves. Hipsters frequent trendy bars, cafes and international restaurants that range from casual to fine dining

Shopping and Entertainment

Central to this area are the following two venues...

Kensington Market on Kensington Ave is a long-standing, colourful market with independent shops/cafes, plus produce, meat & fish stands. The Market is also home to a wide array of specialty grocers, bakeries and cheese shops.

Chinatown Centre on Spadina is a Toronto Chinatown landmark. The Chinatown Centre is a one stop shop, multi-level shopping complex with exclusive specialty boutiques and services.

The Greens Vegetarian Restaurant on Dundas is a simple space serving popular homestyle Chinese, Vietnamese & Thai dishes made with mock meat.

Horseshoe Tavern on Queen just east of Spadina, has an unpretentious front bar with pool table, plus an historic back room with local & touring music acts. The Cameron House is an intimate, bohemian bar on Queen St just west of Spadina, with ceiling murals & nightly performances from local roots acts on 2 stages.

The Entertainment District and Fashion District are just east of here with TIFF Bell Lightbox, Scotiabank Theatre and more. Exhibition Place and the Lake are south of here within easy access. Art Gallery of Ontario just east of here on Dundas is a large gallery with huge Canadian collection, European masterworks & a major Frank Gehry renovation.

Transportation

This area is well served by transit – Queen, Dundas and College streetcars east-west, Bathurst and Spadina streetcars and Union subway line north-south. Union station, Billy Bishop airport, Lakeshore/Gardiner all close by.

Parks

Alexandra Park on Bathurst St has an outdoor pool, a wading pool, an artificial ice rink and tennis courts. Scadding Court Community Centre on the north side of Alexandra Park includes a gymnasium, an indoor pool, a weight room, and meeting rooms.

Adjacent to the community centre is the Charles R. Sanderson Public Library, with programs for adults, children and preschoolers. Grange Park is off Beverley St, near the Art Gallery of Ontario.

More Neighbourhood Features

Toronto Western Hospital is at Bathurst and Dundas.

Who Might Love Living Here And Why

If you work in one of the hospitals along University or downtown or love an ethnic neighbourhood, this neighbourhood might fit your needs.

Downside To Living Here

Traffic on Spadina, crowds in the market

What's The Real Estate Market Like Here

This neighbourhood has the lowest number of sales for 2017 with the vast majority being 1- or 1+den suites. There's not much new construction going on at the moment.

2017 SOLD Statistics For C01 Kensington-Chinatown

Suite Size Options

2017 Units By Size	C01 – Kensington - Chinatown	% Of market
# of bachelor units SOLD	2	1%
# of 1-and 1+den SOLD	92	63%
# of 2-bedrooms SOLD	50	34%
# of 3-bedrooms SOLD	3	6%
TOTAL UNIT SALES=>	147	

Suite Sales #'s Score = 1

What Kind Of Inventory Is There?

2017 Sales by PRICE Range	C01 - Kensington - Chinatown	% Of market
$300-399K	17	12%
$400-499K	45	31%
$500-599K	31	21%
$600-699K	25	17%
$700-799K	9	6%
$800-899K	10	7%
$900-999K	6	4%
$1M – 1.5M	2	1%
$1.5M PLUS	0	0%
Total Sales Between $400,000 and $600,000 = 52%		

Affordability - Average Sale Price (Scored on a 1-5 scale, 5 being highest)

	C01 - Kensington - Chinatown
Running Average Sale Price	$482,809

Affordability Score = 4

Best Appreciation (Scored on a 1-5 scale, 5 being highest)

	C01 - Kensington - Chinatown
Average Y-O-Y Sale Price Change From 2016	19%

Appreciation Score = 1

Best Investment Conclusion (Scored on a 1-5 scale, 5 being highest)

My investment conclusion is based on sales numbers, average purchase price, appreciation history, location downtown and rental potential in each TREB sub-district.

Although its location is very central, this neighbourhood scored lowest on appreciation and second lowest on unit sales. Because of this I've scored it as follows…

Investment Score = 1

CHAPTER 7
C01 SUB-DISTRICT
LITTLE PORTUGAL

Little Portugal

Area Boundaries & Housing Mix

The geographical boundaries of Little Portugal are from Dovercourt Road going west to the train tracks and from Queen West north to College Street.

Little Portugal is a neighbourhood and ethnic enclave in Toronto where many Portuguese emigrated to back in the 1960's and 70's and other ethnicities before that.

Much of the housing stock is semi- and detached homes built back in the late 1800's and early 1900's but new condo buildings have been infilling along the major street for several years now.

Walk & Transit Score

Using the condo building at 998 College St West at the NW corner of Rusholme Road,

Best LOCAL Features

Shopping and Entertainment

A lot of the local buzz is from smaller shops, cafes and restaurants along Queen West, Dundas St West and College.

Dufferin Mall, just to the north on Dufferin, is a sprawling, contemporary shopping centre with big-box anchor stores & brand-name clothing stores.

For entertainment there is the renovated historical Gladstone Hotel on Queen East with chic, individually decorated rooms & suites with a relaxed cafe & a trendy bar. Also, the Lula Lounge on Dundas which hosts local & international acts for salsa, jazz & world music plus has Latin dining & dancing on weekends.

As well, you find the Dog & Bear Pub on Queen, a traditional tavern for beers on tap, classic British pub fare & major sports events on TV, and the Lockhart, which is inspired by the "Harry Potter" novels. This cozy, exposed-brick haunt on Dundas conjures up cocktails & tapas.

The Canadian National Exhibition grounds with annual home shows, the CNE, and the BMO soccer field, are just south of here. For sports and leisure, there is the Boulevard Club on Lake Shore Blvd W, a lakefront, multi-sport club providing lifelong quality programs and services for members.

Transportation

Public transit is readily available via the King, Queen and College streetcars, and there's easy expressway access to the Gardiner Expressway and Lakeshore Blvd West.

Parks

On the lakefront is Sunnyside Park and outdoor swimming pool. And McCormack Park is on Sheridan Ave.

To the west is the sprawling High Park, running from Bloor St down to the Queensway, with hiking trails, a zoo, sports fields & a large children's playground. Located just east of here is Trinity-Bellwoods Park, a spacious park with indoor and outdoor facilities and the Trinity Bellwoods Farmers Market.

Lakeshore Blvd parklands along the lake can be easily accessed just south of here.

More Neighbourhood Features

The closest hospital is St. Joseph's Health Centre on the Queensway.

Who Might Love Living Here And Why

Families, large and small, (lots of parks and recreation) as well as singles and couples (lots of entertainment) who like to live in an established community. Although there's easy access to downtown, you're still outside of the busy core.

Downside To Living Here

Crowds during the Canadian National Exhibition every August looking for parking.

What's The Real Estate Market Like Here

This neighbourhood is slow to develop a strong condominium presence but has a very strong house market.

2017 SOLD Statistics For C01 Little Portugal

Suite Size Options

2017 Units By Size	C01 – Little Portugal	% Of market
# of bachelor units SOLD	0	0%
# of 1-and 1+den SOLD	121	55%
# of 2-bedrooms SOLD	99	45%
# of 3-bedrooms SOLD	0	0%
TOTAL UNIT SALES=>	220	

Suite Sales #'s Score = 2

What Kind Of Inventory Is There?

2017 Sales by PRICE Range	C01 - Little Portugal	% Of market
$300-399K	65	30%
$400-499K	84	39%
$500-599K	42	19%
$600-699K	18	8%
$700-799K	5	2%
$800-899K	2	1%
$900-999K	0	0%
$1M – 1.5M	1	0%
$1.5M PLUS	0	0%
Total Sales Between $400,000 and $600,000 = 58%		

Affordability - Average Sale Price (Scored on a 1-5 scale, 5 being highest)

	C01 - Little Portugal
Running Average Sale Price	$460,704

Affordability Score = 5

Best Appreciation (Scored on a 1-5 scale, 5 being highest)

	C01 - Little Portugal
Average Y-O-Y Sale Price Change From 2016	23%

Appreciation Score = 2

Best Investment Conclusion (Scored on a 1-5 scale, 5 being highest)

My investment conclusion is based on sales numbers, average purchase price, appreciation history, location downtown and rental potential in each TREB sub-district.

This sub-district gets a mid-point investment score of 3. Although Appreciation and Unit Sales scores are low, it scored highest for Affordability.

Investment Score = 3

CHAPTER 8
C08 SUB-DISTRICT
WATERFRONT COMMUNITIES
DISTILLERY DISTRICT, CANARY DISTRICT, RIVER CITY, ST LAWRENCE MARKET, HARBOURFRONT EAST

Waterfront Communities C08

The C08 Waterfront Communities sub-district is comprised of five neighbourhoods, four of which were either developed over the past several years (Distillery District, Canary District and River City) or are just starting to take shape now (Harbourfront East).

All five neighbourhoods included in the Waterfront C08 Communities are located east of Yonge Street over to the Don Valley Parkway (DVP) and stretch from Lake Ontario north to Front St / Eastern Avenue as it crosses the Don River.

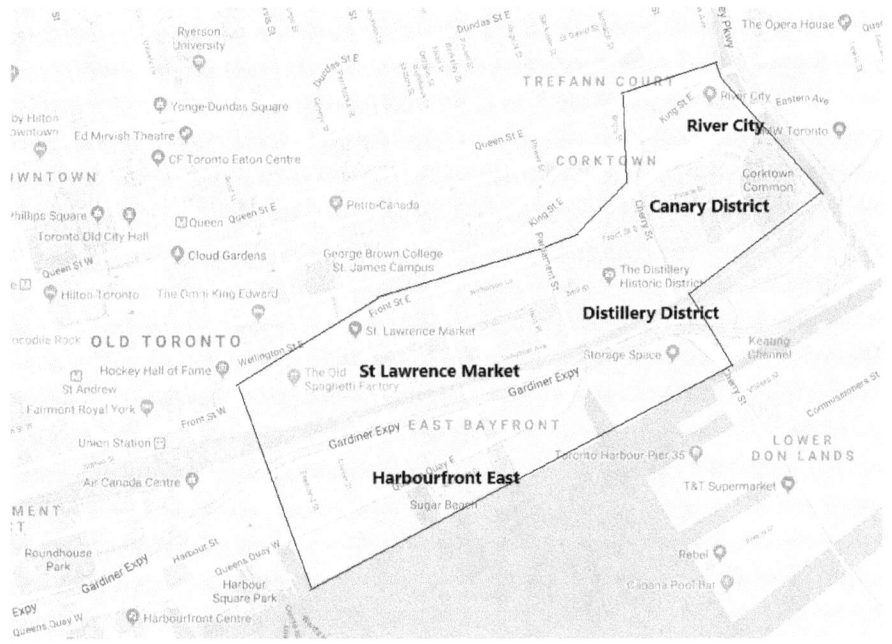

Distillery District Neighbourhood

Area Boundaries & Housing Mix

This special section of downtown Toronto is bordered by Parliament Street on the east and Cherry Street on the west, and further nestled between the Gardiner Expressway and Mill Street.

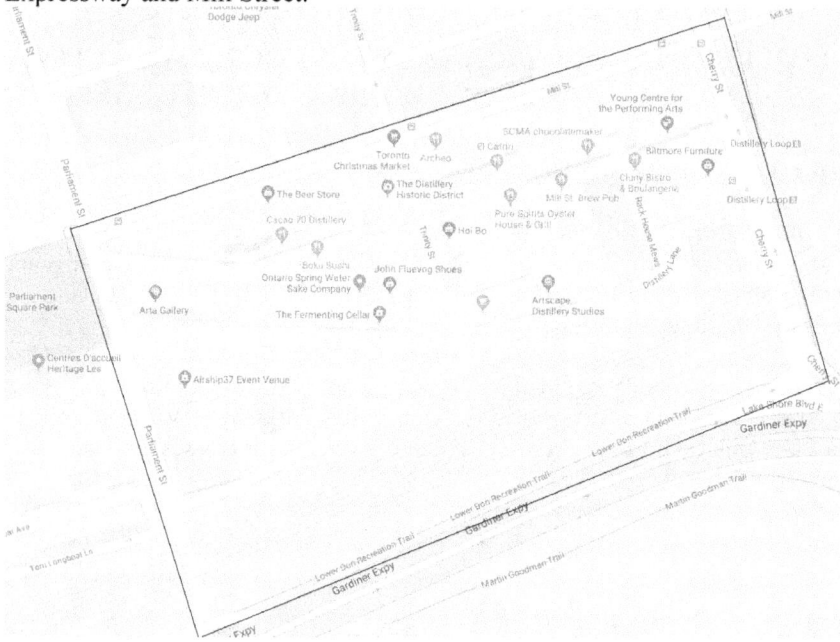

The commercial activity is wrapped around by a series of low- and high-rise condominiums providing an anchor to the neighbourhood with more residences planned for the years ahead. It is a dramatic fusion of old and new. An inspired blend of Victorian Industrial architecture and stunning 21st century design and creativity.

Walk & Transit Score

Using 33 Mill St…

Best LOCAL Features

Shopping and Entertainment

The Distillery is now a meeting place all year round, comprising more than forty heritage buildings and ten streets, and is a large collection of Victorian-era industrial architecture. Located east of downtown, it contains an excellent mix of stores, restaurants, numerous cafés, offices housed within heritage buildings of the former Gooderham and Worts Distillery.

There is also an eclectic mix of street fairs, light shows and entertainment for people of all ages. With more than 80 shops and boutiques, The Distillery District is Toronto's destination for fresh urban style and unique home furnishings. For dining, you find mouth-watering treats from cozy comfort food to French Fusion cuisine.

Transportation

Public transit is available north-south on Parliament St and east-west on King St. If you drive to work downtown and the lakeshore is busy, Richmond will get you there and Adelaide will get you home. The Lakeshore/Gardiner is just down the street and the DVP is around the corner.

Parks

Parliament Square Park is a nice greenspace on the west side of Parliament, and the greenspace continues right over to Jarvis. David Crombie Park sits right in the middle at Lower Sherbourne. To the east, greenspace starts at Mill St and Rolling Mills Rd and continues over to Corktown Common on the east side of Bayview. Also found here, the Lower Don River Trail and Underpass Park.

Go straight down Cherry St to the lake where you find Cherry Beach with a separate off-leash dog park. Tommy Thompson Park is on the Leslie St Spit, and is a car-free nature preserve with numerous bird and small animal species to enjoy.

More Neighbourhood Features

The Studio District is close by, just across the Don.

Who Might Love Living Here And Why

Young professionals, singles, couples, empty-nesters who would like a maintenance free condo lifestyle and lots to do, Artisans, artists inspired by the art fairs and displays in the Distillery.

The Distillery District is a place where creativity flourishes and where artists, artisans, entrepreneurs and businesspeople rub shoulders and inspire each other.

Downside To Living Here

Crowds on weekends or during special events.

What's The Real Estate Market Like Here

People love living here. You're living in the middle of an historic district, so condo suites sell quickly.

Canary District Neighbourhood

Area Boundaries & Housing Mix

The Canary District is bounded by Cherry Street to the west and extends east to the Don River and from the railway tracks to the north of the Gardiner Expressway up to Eastern Avenue.

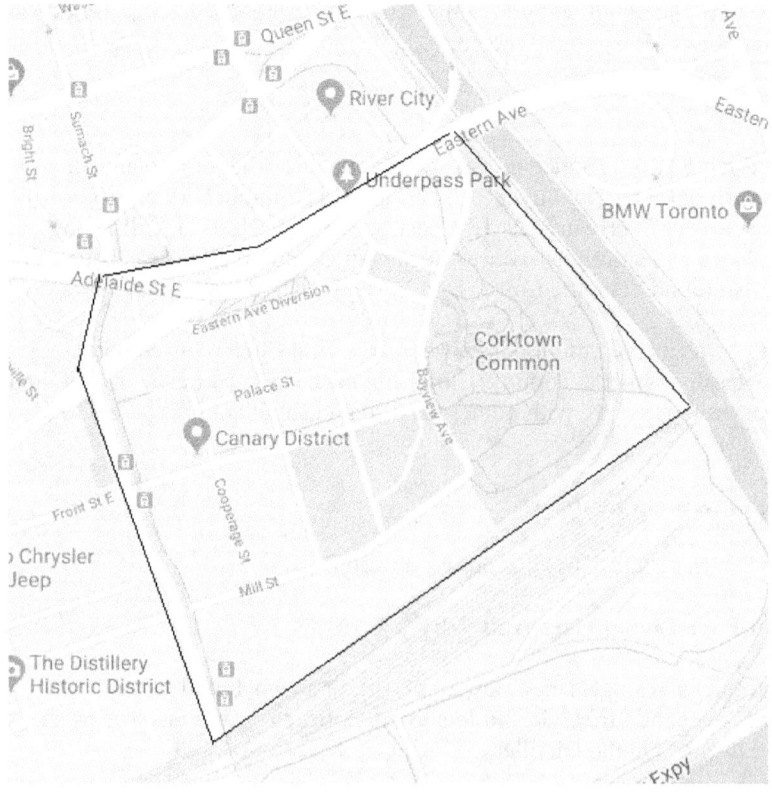

The Canary District is brand new as of the summer Pan-Am games back in 2015 when the residences built for the athletes were converted over, as planned, to condominium suites.

The Canary District was named after a long-time famous greasy-spoon (The Canary) that was located in a century-old building along Cherry Street.

Since 2015, construction of new condos has continued, and new releases are coming each year. The developers have also added a student residence for George Brown College (The George) and a beautiful, brand new Cooper Koo YMCA along with commercial spaces along Front Street East.

Walk & Transit Score

Using the Canary District condos at 398 Front Street East…

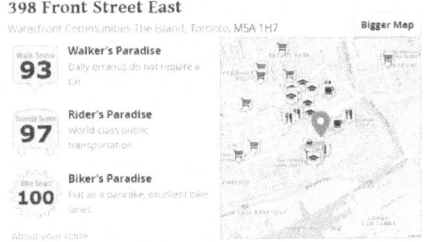

Best LOCAL Features

Shopping and Entertainment

There are excellent businesses in place now with more to come as space comes available. The anchor is the beautiful Cooper Koo YMCA which is at the NE corner of Cherry and Front St East.

Transportation

There are direct streetcar links from the Distillery Loop on Cherry south of Front which will take you straight downtown along King St East and West. The Gardiner / Lakeshore and DVP are all easily accessible.

Parks

Greenspace starts at Mill St and Rolling Mills Rd and continues over to Corktown Common on the east side of Bayview. Also found here, the Lower Don River Trail and Underpass Park.

Over to the west towards downtown, Parliament Square Park is a nice greenspace on the west side of Parliament, and the greenspace continues right over to Jarvis. David Crombie Park sits right in the middle at Lower Sherbourne.

Go straight down Cherry St to the lake where you find Cherry Beach with a separate off-leash dog park. Tommy Thompson Park is on the Leslie St Spit, and is a car-free nature preserve with numerous bird and small animal species to enjoy.

More Neighbourhood Features

The Distillery District is just to the west, and the Studio District is close by, just across the Don.

Who Might Love Living Here And Why

Young professionals, singles, couples, empty-nesters will enjoy a maintenance free condo lifestyle with lots to do locally. Residents can be inspired by the art fairs, restaurants, shops and entertainment taking place in the Distillery District right next door.

Downside To Living Here

There will be some ongoing construction happening over the next few years.

What's The Real Estate Market Like Here

Busy, just like the rest of the downtown condo market. Remember, everything is very new so you've got a big variety of condo suite styles and sizes available to look at.

River City Neighbourhood

Area Boundaries & Housing Mix

River City is also a brand-new neighbourhood pocket stretching from Eastern Avenue north to Queen East and from Sumach Street east to the Don River.

Guide To Downtown Toronto Condo Prices

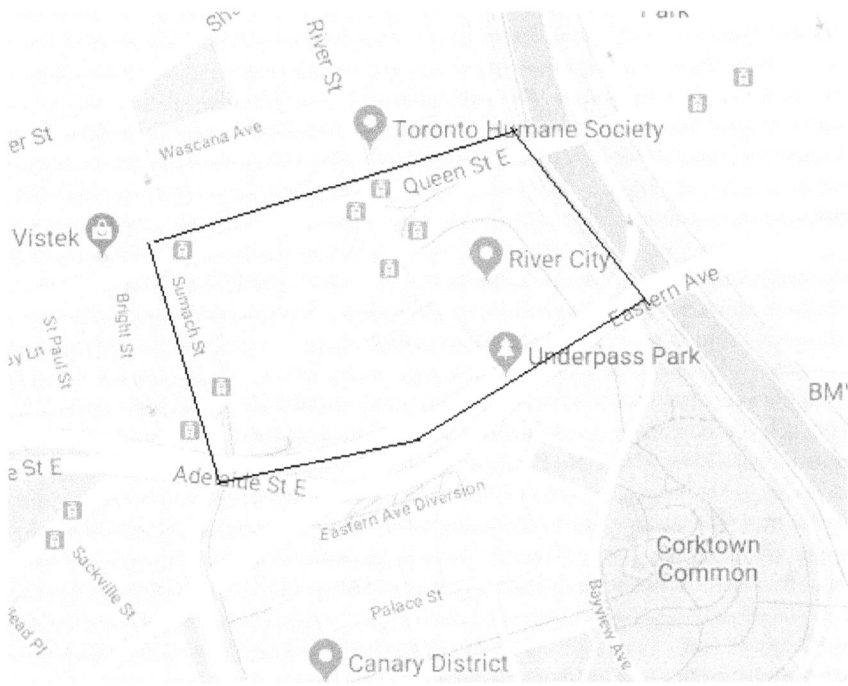

It's a mix of condominium high rise suite and low-rise townhouses.

Walk & Transit Score

Using the River City Lofts at 51 Trolley Crescent as a measuring point…

Best LOCAL Features

Shopping and Entertainment

Downtown, and the areas just east of downtown are a hop, skip and a jump away by car or transit for great shopping and entertainment. From here you have very easy access to more shopping and entertainment, lots of local restaurants and neighbourhood shops along Queen over the Don into the eastern part of the city.

Transportation

There is easy driving access to downtown along Richmond and back along Adelaide or you can take either the King or the Queen streetcars. The DVP and Lakeshore / Gardiner are nearby to give you easy highway access.

Parks

The Lower Don River Trail and Underpass Park are found in this area. More greenspace starts at Mill St and Rolling Mills Rd and continues over to Corktown Common on the east side of Bayview.

Over to the west towards downtown, Parliament Square Park is a nice greenspace on the west side of Parliament, and the greenspace continues right over to Jarvis. David Crombie Park sits right in the middle at Lower Sherbourne.

Go straight down Cherry St to the lake where you find Cherry Beach with a separate off-leash dog park. Tommy Thompson Park is on the Leslie St Spit, and is a car-free nature preserve with numerous bird and small animal species to enjoy.

More Neighbourhood Features

The Distillery and Canary Districts are just south.

Who Might Love Living Here And Why

Young professionals, singles, couples, empty-nesters will enjoy a maintenance free condo lifestyle with lots to do.

You'll also be east of the downtown traffic but close enough to even bike or walk to work or play.

Just east across the bridge there are all the great stores and restaurants from the South Riverdale neighbourhood.

Downside To Living Here

There will be new condo construction going on for a few years yet.

What's The Real Estate Market Like Here

Brand new construction is causing the cost per square foot to rise for resale suites.

St Lawrence Market

Area Boundaries & Housing Mix

My somewhat arbitrary definition is from Yonge Street east to Parliament and from the train tracks north to Front Street.

Walk & Transit Score

Using, on the east side, the Yorktown On The Park suites at 222 The Esplanade and on the western end, the Esplanade Condos at 25 The Esplanade

Best LOCAL Features

Shopping and Entertainment

The St Lawrence Market neighbourhood has a seemingly endless list of things to do.

The St Lawrence Market itself is Toronto's oldest market with 100+ vendors, bakers, butchers & artisans, with lots of folks shopping for their next week's dinners.

For theatre, the Sony Centre for the Performing Arts on Front St is a spacious, storied venue with elegant decor hosting concerts, theatre performances & cultural events.

The Air Canada Centre just west of here on the lower part of Bay St is a large arena hosting pro hockey, basketball & lacrosse, plus many visiting big-name music acts.

C'est What is a subterranean taproom on Front St offering comfort food plus dozens of craft beers, a whisky bar & board games and great music.

Sukhothai is a very popular Thai restaurant on Wellington where husband-and-wife owners serve classic Thai fare, from spring rolls to curries, in a casual setting.

Transportation

The TTC runs east-west along The Esplanade and King, and there is TTC north-south along Lower Sherbourne that loops around Lower Jarvis below the Esplanade, right in the middle of this neighbourhood. There is TTC north-south on Parliament on the east side, and the Yonge St subway line on the west side. Lakeshore / Gardiner access is very close, as is the DVP. Union Station sits to the southwest of here.

Parks

Over to the west towards downtown, Parliament Square Park is a nice greenspace on the west side of Parliament, and the greenspace continues right over to Jarvis. David Crombie Park sits right in the middle at Lower Sherbourne.

Berczy Park sits nestled between Wellington, Front and Scott, and with its centrepiece fountain and benches, is a popular place to sit and enjoy the hustle and bustle of the people enjoying this fabulous neighbourhood, as well as the picturesque view of the buildings along Front St.

Go straight down Sherbourne to Lakeshore Blvd, where you will find Sherbourne Common stretching down to the lake, and Sugar Beach just a bit west at the lake.

More Neighbourhood Features

The Distillery Historic District lies on the eastern boundary.

Who Might Love Living Here And Why

Everyone young and old! Everyone... young professionals, singles, couples and empty-nesters will enjoy a maintenance free downtown condo lifestyle with lots to do.

You've got easy walking access to everything downtown Toronto offers.

Downside To Living Here

Traffic on Jarvis to get to the Gardiner is very busy in year round

What's The Real Estate Market Like Here

Just like everywhere else when you're close to the centre of the city, there's high demand.

Harbourfront EAST Neighbourhood

Area Boundaries & Housing Mix

The borders of Harbourfront EAST are from Lake Ontario north to the railway tracks and from Yonge Street east to Cherry Street.

Until the Pier 27 condos were first built at 29 and 39 Queens Quay East several years ago, there were no residences east of Yonge.

Now there are several new buildings close to completion and many more either on the drawing boards or under construction.

Walk & Transit Score

Using the **Pier 27 condos at 39 Queens Quay East**,

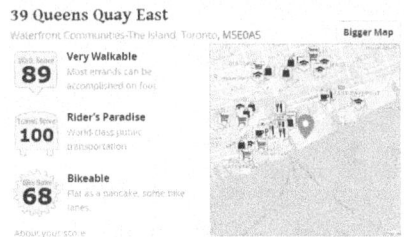

Best LOCAL Features

The lake... the lake and the lake!!

As more condo suites and office buildings are constructed, expect this neighbourhood to boom as more people live and work in the area.

Shopping and Entertainment

Harbourfront is conveniently located within walking distance of the St. Lawrence Market, Toronto's oldest and largest food market.

A giant Loblaws food and retail centre is located on Queens Quay at the foot of Jarvis Street. Markets, bars and restaurant with patios, grocery stores and other shopping destinations at Harbourfront West round off the Harbourfront as one of Toronto's most sought-after neighbourhoods to live and play in.

Transportation

At present there's a TTC bus service along Queen's Quay East taking you to Union Station with a connection with the subway and streetcar service west from that point.

Parks

The bicycle / walking trail already extends from one end of Queens Quay East to the other and connects with the Martin Goodman Trail.

More Neighbourhood Features

Points of interest nearby include the Redpath Sugar Museum, art galleries, the Spadina Quay wetlands, the Fort York National Historic Site and Exhibition Place.

Who Might Love Living Here And Why

Adventurers… millennials… empty nesters… any and all ages love access to the Lake Ontario views any season of the year. Although it's a bit 'industrial' now, the future looks fantastic for this neighbourhood with a lot better planning than happened west of Yonge.

Downside To Living Here

So far, the public transit connection is a bus service but streetcars are expected to be added in the next few years. There's going to be construction going on down here for several years to come.

What's The Real Estate Market Like Here

So far, with the exception of Pier 27, it's all developer pre-construction sales but expect that to change once the next few condo buildings take occupancy sometime this year.

2017 SOLD Statistics For C08 Waterfront Communities (East)

Suite Size Options

2017 Units By Size	C08 – Waterfront	% Of market
# of bachelor units SOLD	6	2%
# of 1-and 1+den SOLD	230	59%
# of 2-bedrooms SOLD	147	38%
# of 3-bedrooms SOLD	6	2%
TOTAL UNIT SALES=>	389	

Suite Sales #'s Score = 4

What Kind Of Inventory Is There?

2017 Sales by PRICE Range	C08 - Waterfront	% Of market
$300-399K	23	6%
$400-499K	87	22%
$500-599K	99	25%
$600-699K	75	19%
$700-799K	50	13%
$800-899K	19	5%
$900-999K	13	3%
$1M – 1.5M	15	4%
$1.5M PLUS	8	2%
Total Sales Between $400,000 and $600,000 = 47%		

Affordability - Average Sale Price (Scored on a 1-5 scale, 5 being highest)

	C08 - Waterfront
Running Average Sale Price	$647,997

Affordability Score = 2

Best Appreciation (Scored on a 1-5 scale, 5 being highest)

	C08 - Waterfront
Average Y-O-Y Sale Price Change From 2016	25%

Appreciation Score = 5

Best Investment Conclusion (Scored on a 1-5 scale, 5 being highest)

My investment conclusion is based on sales numbers, average purchase price, appreciation history, location downtown and rental potential in each TREB sub-district.

Although the Appreciation Score was high, the Unit Sales were middle of the pack and Affordability was almost the lowest of all the C08 sub-districts.

Investment Score = 3

CHAPTER 9
C08 SUB-DISTRICT
CHURCH-YONGE CORRIDOR

Church-Yonge Corridor

Area Boundaries & Housing Mix

The Church-Yonge corridor stretches from Front Street East north to Bloor and from Yonge Street east to Jarvis Street.

Guide To Downtown Toronto Condo Prices

Although there are plenty of lovely semi and detached houses and townhouses dating back to the late 1800's, a lot of infill condominium buildings have been constructed in the last 15+ years.

Condo buyers here are sure to find this neighourhood has plenty of charm and character. There are a variety of buildings to suit any lifestyle from both high- and low-rise condo buildings.

Walk & Transit Score

Using the 88 Scott Street Condos near the south end of the corridor, and to the north, the X2 Condos at 101 Charles St East

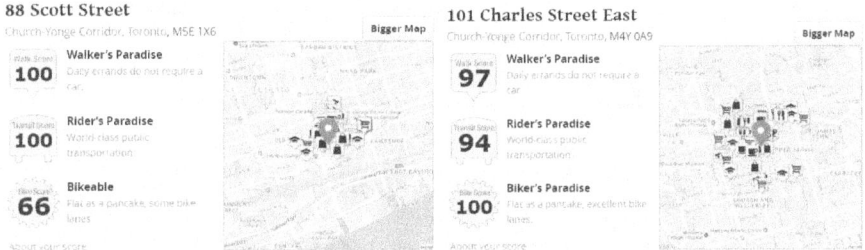

Best LOCAL Features

Shopping and Entertainment

The Church and Wellesley area, a hub for Toronto's LGBT community, is centrally located within the Corridor, which is also home to a number of great shopping and entertainment opportunities, including College Park, the Church Street Diner, Massey Hall and the Elgin Theatre. The Carlton Cinema is a multiplex on Carlton, with film-themed art showing Hollywood, independent, Canadian & foreign flicks.

Yonge-Dundas Square is a bustling outdoor public space & live-event venue hosting concerts, movies & community events at Yonge and Dundas.

Transportation

You're right in the middle of everything! The Church-Yonge Corridor is heavily serviced by public transit with buses, streetcars and subway routes on both the Yonge line and the Bloor-Danforth line.

Parks

This area is also home to a number of green spaces and landmarks, including Allan Gardens, St James Park and Cawthra Square.

More Neighbourhood Features

Sunnybrook Hospital is on Wellesley between Yonge and Church. Ryerson University on Victoria St is an urban, career-oriented public research university known for programs such as engineering & business.

Who Might Love Living Here And Why

This long strip of neighbourhood in downtown Toronto is lively and full of character and is home to a complete mix of people of differing ethnic backgrounds, ages and socioeconomic status.

Singles, couples, families, students and professionals all make their homes here, and there's no shortage of things to do no matter who you are with communities such as Yorkville and the Distillery District plus the University of Toronto, and Ryerson campus' very close by.

Downside To Living Here

Yonge Street has a lot of new construction happening which will last several more years.

What's The Real Estate Market Like Here

This whole area is booming with infill condominium buildings to complement the suites that have been added over the last 15+ years and demand is high for both.

2017 SOLD Statistics For C08 Church-Yonge Corridor

Suite Size Options

2017 Units By Size	C08 – Church-Yonge Corridor	% Of market
# of bachelor units SOLD	46	5%
# of 1-and 1+den SOLD	515	58%
# of 2-bedrooms SOLD	327	37%
# of 3-bedrooms SOLD	7	1%
TOTAL UNIT SALES=>	895	

Suite Sales #'s Score = 5

What Kind Of Inventory Is There?

2017 Sales by PRICE Range	C08 – Church-Yonge Corridor	% Of market
$300-399K	71	8%
$400-499K	242	27%
$500-599K	201	22%
$600-699K	150	17%
$700-799K	86	10%
$800-899K	57	6%
$900-999K	40	4%
$1M – 1.5M	35	4%
$1.5M PLUS	12	1%
Total Sales Between $400,000 and $600,000 = 49%		

Affordability - Average Sale Price (Scored on a 1-5 scale, 5 being highest)

	C08 - Church-Yonge Corridor
Running Average Sale Price	$621,618

Affordability Score = 3

Best Appreciation (Scored on a 1-5 scale, 5 being highest)

	C08 - Church-Yonge Corridor
Average Y-O-Y Sale Price Change From 2016	25%

Appreciation Score = 5

Best Investment Conclusion (Scored on a 1-5 scale, 5 being highest)

My investment conclusion is based on sales numbers, average purchase price, appreciation history, location downtown and rental potential in each TREB sub-district.

Because of the top scores for Appreciation and Unit Sales and despite a middle-point Affordability score, I've rated it a 5.

Investment Score = 5

CHAPTER 10
C08 SUB-DISTRICT
MOSS PARK

Moss Park

Area Boundaries & Housing Mix

Moss Park stretches from Jarvis east to Parliament and from Front St East north to Carlton.

In the past several years, builders have taken advantage of lower land prices east of Yonge to start infilling and that continues today. So far most of the new construction has taken place at the southern end of this district but expect more to come farther north as the easy-to-build-on sites are completed.

Walk & Transit Score

Using, The Richmond condos at 313 Richmond Street East

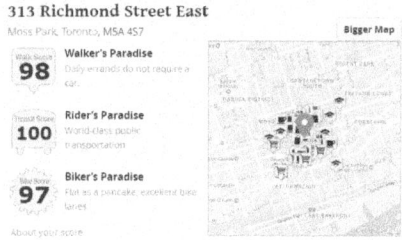

Best LOCAL Features

Shopping and Entertainment

There is local shopping on Front, King, Queen and Parliament Streets. The biggest grocery store nearby is the Loblaws at Carlton and Church… the original site of Maple Leaf Gardens. The Eaton Centre on Yonge, stretching from Queen to Dundas is within walking distance.

Just north of Carlton, on Sherbourne is the Phoenix Concert Theatre, a spacious standing-room-only concert venue with 3 separate rooms, several bars & weekend dancing.

Ed Mirvish Theatre, Elgin and Winter Garden Theatre Centre, offer great performances, Massey Hall is a music venue with renowned acoustics that has hosted legendary shows. They are all just west of here, between Queen and Dundas.

Transportation

There are east-west streetcars on Carlton, Dundas, Queen and King, as well as north-south buses running on Parliament and Sherbourne. There is easy DVP access, as well as highway access via Lakeshore Blvd and the Gardiner Expressway to the south.

Parks

Allan Gardens is the large park at the north end of this area. The park surrounds the Botanical Garden, which is a collection of plants from around the world housed in a cast-iron & glass building dating to 1910.

St. James Park is a series of formal gardens located next to St. James Cathedral is just west of Jarvis, north of King St. This is a beautiful place to stroll and relax, with a grand gazebo in the centre of the park, and walking trails traversing the grass and tree dotted area.

More Neighbourhood Features

Ryerson University, just west of Church and Dundas, is an urban, career-oriented public research university known for programs such as engineering & business. Ryerson University Library & Archives is located at the north end of the university.

Who Might Love Living Here And Why

Single professionals and young couples who work downtown and empty nesters who want to be close to downtown but live just outside of the high-traffic neighbourhoods will love living here.

Downside To Living Here

It's still a bit 'rough' around the intersection of Queen and Sherbourne where hostels draw in a lot of street people etc.

What's The Real Estate Market Like Here

This neighbourhood is getting more popular because it's relatively close to the downtown core (closer than King West or Liberty Village for example).

It's a cascade effect. As more suites are built and occupied, there are more people out on the street. As the number of people increases, new buyers feel better about living there and become more interested in residing or investing in the neighbourhood.

2017 SOLD Statistics For C08 Moss Park

Suite Size Options

2017 Units By Size	C08 – Moss Park	% Of market
# of bachelor units SOLD	9	2%
# of 1-and 1+den SOLD	287	70%
# of 2-bedrooms SOLD	111	27%
# of 3-bedrooms SOLD	3	1%
TOTAL UNIT SALES=>	410	

Suite Sales #'s Score = 4

What Kind Of Inventory Is There?

2017 Sales by PRICE Range	C08 - Moss Park	% Of market
$300-399K	46	11%
$400-499K	119	29%
$500-599K	100	25%
$600-699K	58	14%
$700-799K	43	11%
$800-899K	19	5%
$900-999K	9	2%
$1M – 1.5M	10	2%
$1.5M PLUS	3	1%
Total Sales Between $400,000 and $600,000 = 54%		

Affordability - Average Sale Price (Scored on a 1-5 scale, 5 being highest)

	C08 - Moss Park
Running Average Sale Price	$575,854

Affordability Score = 4

Best Appreciation (Scored on a 1-5 scale, 5 being highest)

	C08 - Moss Park
Average Y-O-Y Sale Price Change From 2016	22%

Appreciation Score = 4

Best Investment Conclusion (Scored on a 1-5 scale, 5 being highest)

My investment conclusion is based on sales numbers, average purchase price, appreciation history, location downtown and rental potential in each TREB sub-district.

Moss Park tied for second place total score with Regent Park and has 54% of its units sold in the $400-600,000 price range. I've scored it a 4.

Investment Score = 4

CHAPTER 11
C08 SUB-DISTRICT
REGENT PARK

Regent Park

Area Boundaries & Housing Mix

Regent Park stretches from Parliament St east to River Street and from Queen East north to Gerrard St East.

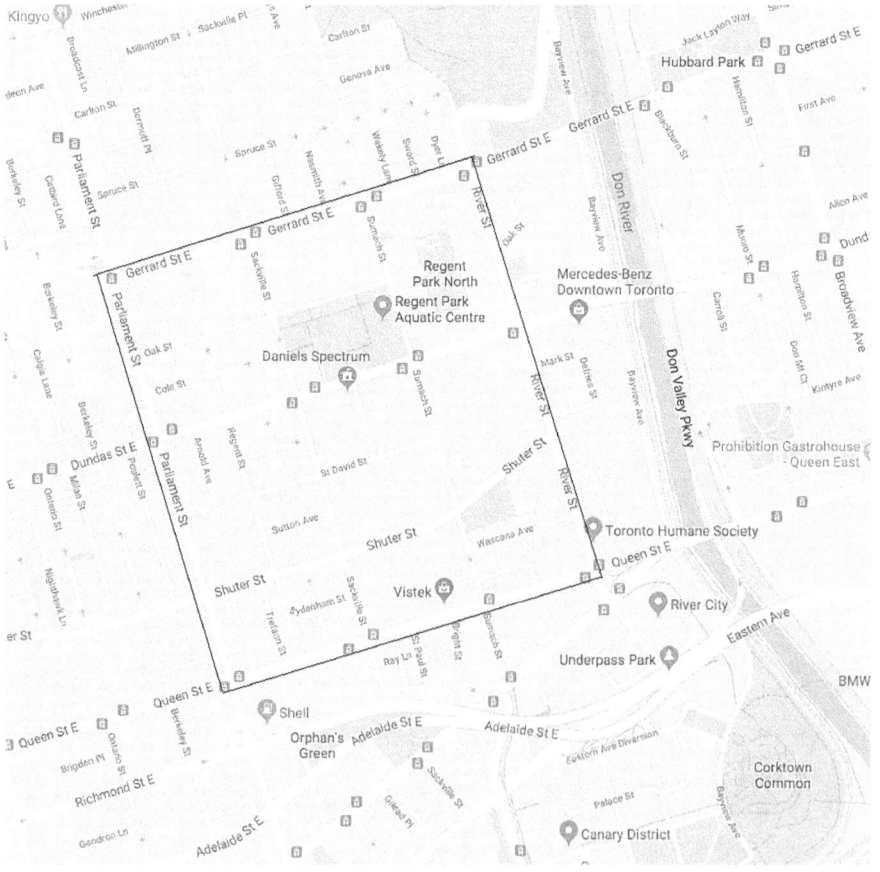

Guide To Downtown Toronto Condo Prices

A promising new chapter in the history of Regent Park is well underway with a revitalization project projected to cost $1 billion and take 15 years to complete. Located in Toronto's thriving Downtown East, Regent Park is bordered by River Street to the east, Queen Street East to the south, Gerrard Street at the north end, and Parliament Street as the western boundary.

This neighbourhood used to have a really bad rap because of the deteriorated social housing but that's almost all gone now.

The 'new' Regent Park consists of a mix of market condos, affordable housing units and vibrant new retail and community space – all freshly built in the last several years and ongoing today.

A key part of the revitalization of Regent Park is to situate both rent-geared-to-income and condo units in the same community. When the revitalization is completed over the next 10 to 15 years, 12,500 people will live in 5,115 units across 69 acres of the largest publicly funded community in Canada.

This includes replacing over 2,000 existing social housing units in Regent Park with new, energy efficient, modern units as well as introducing approximately 3,000 condominium suites for sale.

Walk & Transit Score

Using a central location of the One Cole Condos at 500 Dundas St E

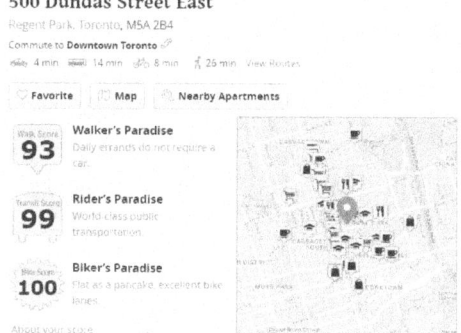

Best LOCAL Features

The revitalization reconnects Regent Park to Toronto's streets and avenues, and includes creating new commercial spaces and community facilities including a bank, grocery store, aquatic centre, new community centre, restaurants and an Arts & Cultural Centre.

Shopping and Entertainment

The downtown hub is minutes away to the west, with theatres, the Eaton Centre, Dundas Square, and lots to do along Yonge St. There are some shops and services located along Gerrard, River, and Parliament Streets. The Distillery Historic District is just south of here.

Daniels Spectrum, a 60,000 sf cultural hub includes the Paintbox Bistro, Regent Park Aquatic Centre, a 6-acre community park, the urban mews on Regent Park Boulevard, the City of Toronto Community Centre and lots of retail stores.

The high-tech, fully accessible Regent Park Aquatic Centre is located on Dundas east of Parliament. It features a lap pool, leisure pool, therapy pool, Tarzan rope, diving board, waterslide, and large sliding glass doors that open onto a sun terrace.

The Regent Park Community Centre is the hub of this community and has a gymnasium, a games room, an arts and crafts room, and a weight room and also includes an employment centre, a teaching kitchen, community hall, meeting rooms and a rooftop garden. The Regent Park Recreation Centre includes a small gymnasium, a meeting room, and an outdoor pool.

Transportation

Streetcars running east-west on Gerrard, Dundas and Queen Streets connect passengers to the Yonge-University-Spadina subway line. The Parliament streetcar connects to Castle Frank station on the Bloor-Danforth subway line.

The Gardiner Expressway / Lake Shore Boulevard and Don Valley Expressway are just minutes away.

Parks

Regent Park has two outdoor artificial ice rinks, a baseball diamond, a swimming pool, and many small parks, some of which contain a children's playground and a wading pool.

The Don River trails, Riverdale Farm and Riverdale Park are just northeast. Nearby to the west is the Garden District. Allan Gardens has a collection of plants from around the world housed in a cast-iron & glass building dating to 1910.

More Neighbourhood Features

There is also a community health centre and a handful of local convenience type stores, located in the middle of Regent Park on Belshaw Place. The Parliament Street Public Library on Gerrard Street East offers a variety of programs for children and adults.

Who Might Love Living Here And Why

Regent Park residents come from a wide variety of cultural backgrounds including many new Canadians from Africa, Asia, and Latin America. There are more than sixty different languages spoken here making the Regent Park neighbourhood one of Toronto's most culturally diverse.

Young professionals, singles and couples will enjoy life in the condos with easy access to downtown, but just away from the busy area.

Also, there is easy access to the east side of the Don River and the film business in the Studio District. For students, Ryerson University and George Brown College are minutes away.

Downside To Living Here

It's a neighbourhood in transition but all for the good. There's still lots of construction going on nearby.

What's The Real Estate Market Like Here

Although just over 170 units sold here in 2017, the average sale price is lower and the housing stock is very new with more coming online every year.

2017 SOLD Statistics For C08 Regent Park

Suite Size Options

2017 Units By Size	C08 – Regent Park	% Of market
# of bachelor units SOLD	4	2%
# of 1-and 1+den SOLD	100	58%
# of 2-bedrooms SOLD	66	39%
# of 3-bedrooms SOLD	1	1%
TOTAL UNIT SALES=>	171	

Suite Sales #'s Score = 2

What Kind Of Inventory Is There?

2017 Sales by PRICE Range	C08 - Regent Park	% Of market
$300-399K	28	16%
$400-499K	70	40%
$500-599K	54	31%
$600-699K	15	9%
$700-799K	1	1%
$800-899K	1	1%
$900-999K	0	0%
$1M – 1.5M	4	2%
$1.5M PLUS	0	0%
Total Sales Between $400,000 and $600,000 = 71%		

Affordability - Average Sale Price (Scored on a 1-5 scale, 5 being highest)

	C08 - Regent Park
Running Average Sale Price	$498,652

Affordability Score = 5

Best Appreciation (Scored on a 1-5 scale, 5 being highest)

This sub-district has one of the highest year-over-year appreciation (Y-O-Y) of any downtown neighbourhood.

	C08 - Regent Park
Average Y-O-Y Sale Price Change From 2016	25%

Appreciation Score = 5

Best Investment Conclusion (Scored on a 1-5 scale, 5 being highest)

My investment conclusion is based on sales numbers, average purchase price, appreciation history, location downtown and rental potential in each TREB sub-district.

Regent Park hit top numbers for both Appreciation and Affordability in 2017. And there are more condo buildings and neighbourhood improvements either under construction or on the drawing boards.

I've scored it a 4.

Investment Score = 4

CHAPTER 12
C02 SUB-DISTRICT
THE ANNEX – YORKVILLE

The Annex-Yorkville

Area Boundaries & Housing Mix

The Yorkville boundaries for the purposes of this analysis are from Yonge St west to St George, and from Bloor St E north to Davenport.

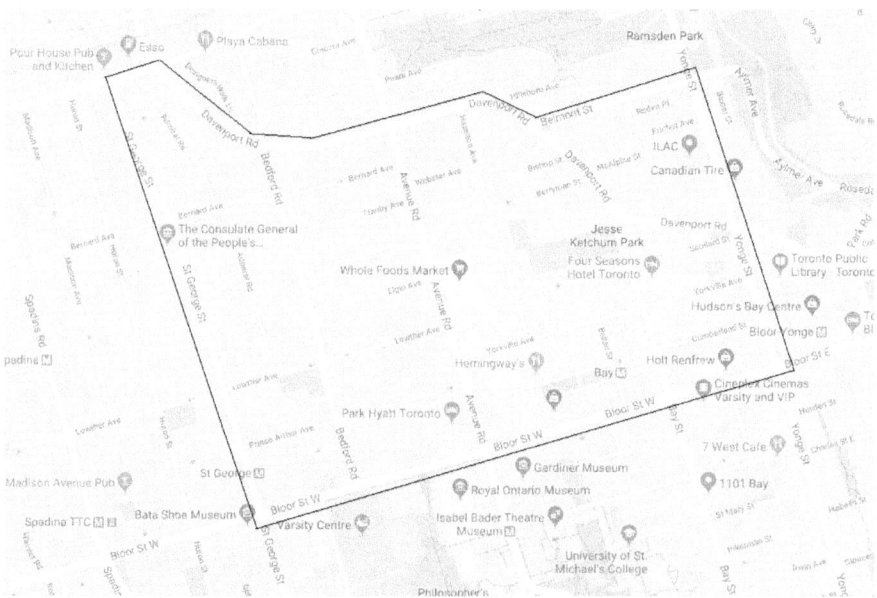

Yorkville is one of Toronto's oldest neighbourhoods and is known for its distinctive houses, and lively happenings along Bloor Street.

Considered by some a food and shopping mecca, Torontonians feel this is one of the friendliest neighbourhoods in the city.

While many side streets are mostly residential, with large, stately mansions to the north of Bloor Street, the area also includes countless detached and semi-detached homes, most built in the elegant Victorian style at the turn of the century, with fine architectural detail.

Guide To Downtown Toronto Condo Prices

Over the past 20+ years, many luxury condo buildings have been added in to the housing mix, especially in and around Yorkville, one of the neighbourhood's most upscale areas.

Walk & Transit Score

Using the 10 Bellair Residences condo building at 10 Bellair,

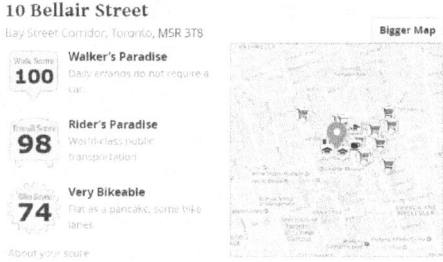

Best LOCAL Features

Luxury shopping and restaurants are the focus in this lively downtown community running north of the University of Toronto. Starting at Yonge Street and going west along Bloor you have the ultra high-end shops and wealth of the stretch along Bloor west to Avenue Rd.

Shopping and Entertainment

Most of the commercial activity in the neighbourhood takes place along Bloor St, one of the busiest areas of town, which is filled with clothing boutiques, small restaurants and outdoor cafes, pubs and bookshops.

The many restaurants, bars and patios offer food and drink from all around the world. Keeping true to Toronto's multicultural flavor, you're likely to find sushi restaurants, pizzerias and falafel stands within a few steps of each other. Whatever you're looking for, you'll likely find it in the Annex.

There is also the ultra-chic Yorkville Avenue and Cumberland Street, each running west from Bay St, where you will find lovely shops and popular restaurants, many of which are visited by celebrities, especially during the Toronto International Film Festival. A well know one is Sassafraz, a fashionable corner dining room with a popular patio, serving French-inspired Canadian cuisine.

Some notables for a cultural afternoon are the Bata Shoe Museum on Bloor at St George, and the Royal Ontario Museum on Queens Park. And, just northwest of here, The Spadina House Museum and Casa Loma.

Transportation

This neighbourhood is well served by public transit. The north-south University-Spadina line runs to Spadina Station from Union Station, and the St George Station on the same line is very handy to this area. The Bloor-Danforth line runs east-west with stops at Spadina, Bay and Yonge. The Spadina station has transfer-free connections to streetcars running south to Queens Quay in Harbourfront. There is a bus along Avenue Rd as well.

The Don Valley Expressway is close by, accessed via Rosedale Valley Rd, from which you can easily go north to Hwy 401 Or south to the Gardiner / Lakeshore.

Parks

Ramsden Park is just north of Belmont off Yonge, And Jesse Ketchum Park runs east off the very North part of Bay Street. The Village of Yorkville Park sits right in the middle of Yorkville.

And then there are the picturesque grounds of the U of T. Philosopher's Walk, which runs south from Bloor and starts between the ROM and the Royal Conservatory. Just south is Queen's Park - The home of Ontario's provincial legislature is another pleasant place to stroll or people-watch.

More Neighbourhood Features

Toronto Public Library - Toronto Reference Library is at Yonge north of Bloor, and Yorkville has its own quaint, much smaller library as well. There is a string of hospitals and medical buildings along University Ave, south of Queens Park, between College and Dundas

Who Might Love Living Here And Why

The Annex is Toronto's most heterogenous community. Its residents include successful business people, prominent artists, University of Toronto students and faculty, and people from all walks of life.

Downside To Living Here

None !!

What's The Real Estate Market Like Here

Although the luxury market is slightly slower at this time, out-of-town buyers find this neighbourhood very interesting as an investment and 'Third-Home' location.

2017 SOLD Statistics For C02 The Annex-Yorkville

Suite Size Options

2017 Units By Size	C02 – The Annex	% Of market
# of bachelor units SOLD	7	3%
# of 1-and 1+den SOLD	108	42%
# of 2-bedrooms SOLD	123	48%
# of 3-bedrooms SOLD	18	7%
TOTAL UNIT SALES=>	256	

Suite Sales #'s Score = 3

What Kind Of Inventory Is There?

2017 Sales by PRICE Range	C02 - The Annex	% Of market
$300-399K	6	2%
$400-499K	26	10%
$500-599K	36	14%
$600-699K	26	10%
$700-799K	25	10%
$800-899K	28	11%
$900-999K	15	6%
$1M – 1.5M	42	16%
$1.5M PLUS	55	21%
Total Sales Between $400,000 and $600,000 = 24%		

Affordability - Average Sale Price (Scored on a 1-5 scale, 5 being highest)

	C02 - The Annex
Running Average Sale Price	$1,232,200

Affordability Score = 1

Best Appreciation (Scored on a 1-5 scale, 5 being highest)

	C02 - The Annex
Average Y-O-Y Sale Price Change From 2016	18%

Appreciation Score = 2

Best Investment Conclusion (Scored on a 1-5 scale, 5 being highest)

My investment conclusion is based on sales numbers, average purchase price, appreciation history, location downtown and rental potential in each TREB sub-district.

The Yorkville Average Sale Price is absolutely the highest of all downtown condo neighbourhoods as expected which unfortunately puts the affordability score right at the bottom of the rankings.

The Total Unit Sales number was the second lowest which may at times prevent liquidity if you want to sell in certain markets.

Investment Score = 2

A FINAL SUMMARY...

Affordability

The C01 District west of Yonge offers more affordable neighbourhoods with four of them above 50% of their total sales being in the $400,000 to $600,000 price range.

However in the C08 sub-district for Regent Park, over 70% of the suites sold are in that 'affordability' range.

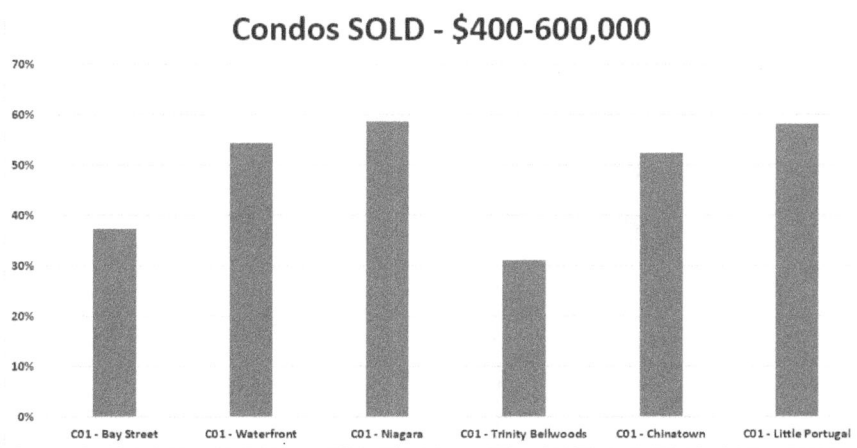

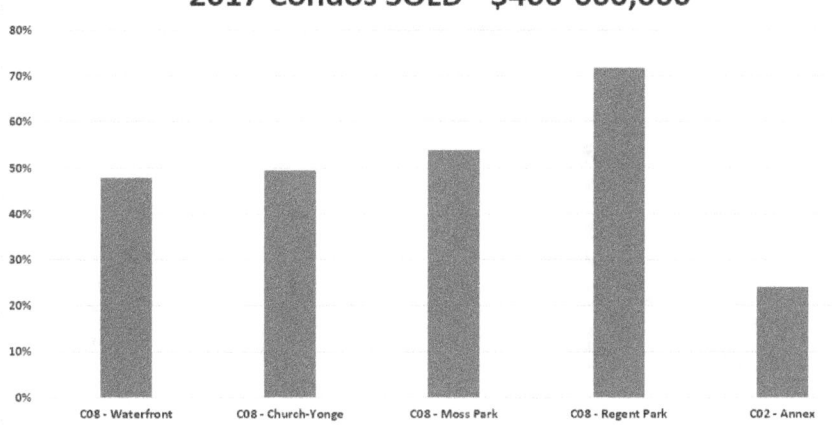

TOTAL Suite Sales

Suite sales in the C01 district are highly concentrated in the southern end of the district and include all the popular neighbourhoods such as the Waterfront, CityPlace, the Entertainment District, King & Queen West, Liberty Village, Fort York and the Bay Street corridor.

The neighbourhoods which are predominantly single family houses only show small condo development so far. This will likely change somewhat with 'main street' infill buildings but are unlikely to catch up in volume with the neighbourhoods previously mentioned.

In C08, the Church-Yonge corridor has the most sales so far but expect this to change as the Waterfront East area gets further developed over the next several years.

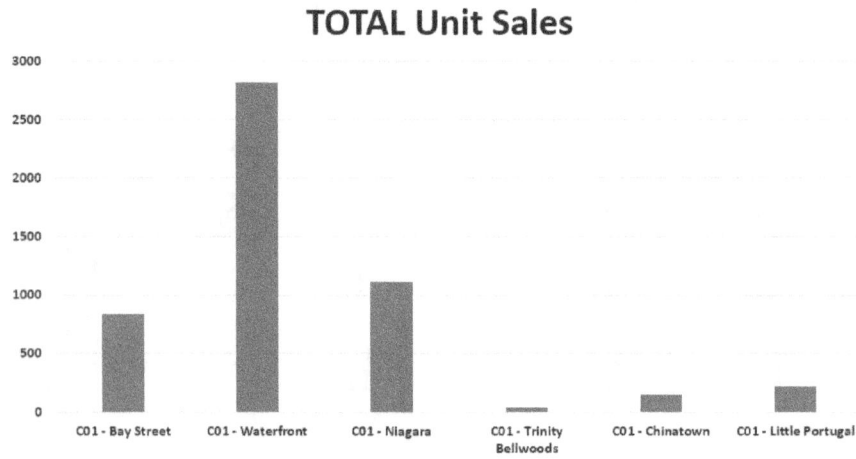

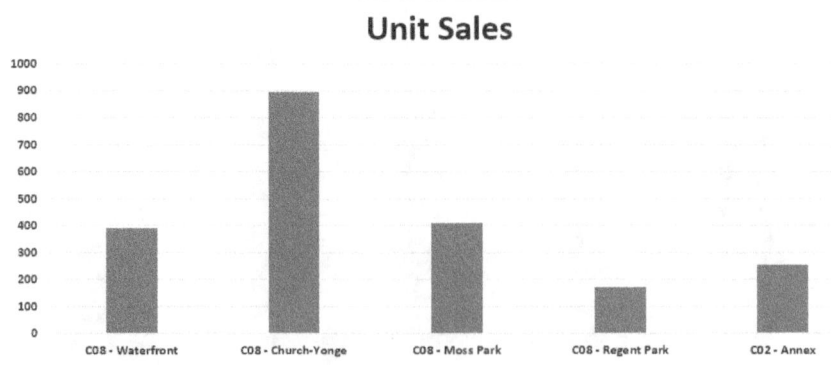

Year-Over-Year Appreciation

Five out of six C01 sub-districts surveyed showed appreciation during 2017 to be above 20%. While Trinity-Bellwoods showed a high 39%, this was mainly due to a small number of unit sales.

All four of C08 sub-districts appeared in the 'above 20%' appreciation level while the luxury neighbourhood of Yorkville came in not too shabby at 18%.

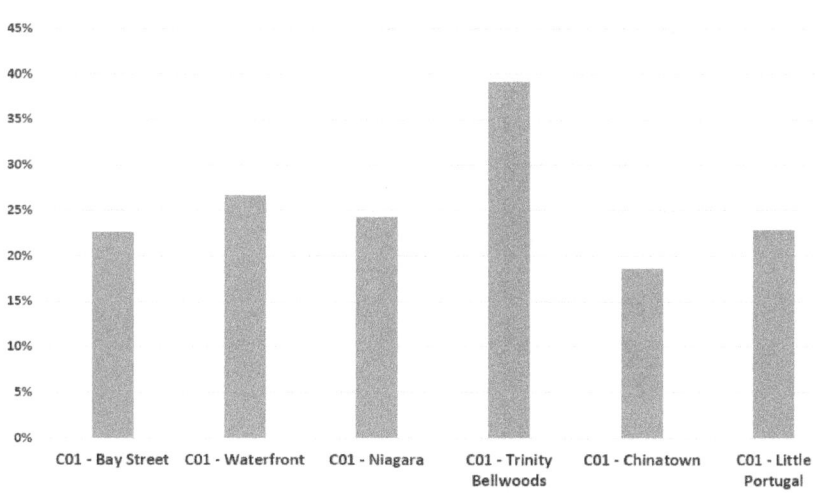

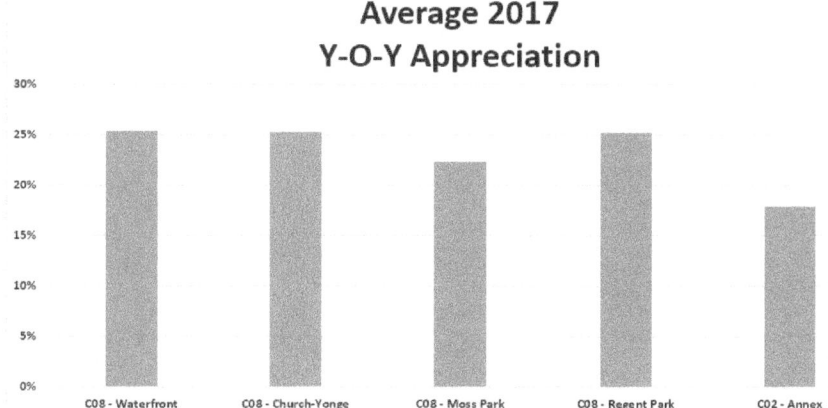

2018 DOWNTOWN CONDO MARKET PROJECTIONS

While downtown Toronto condominium sales volumes will likely be lower in 2018, I expect that the average sale price of downtown condos will continue to increase but in a moderate fashion.

Downtown condominium appreciation levels, while continuing to outpace the overall Toronto/GTA market, will not be as high as they were in 2017.

I'd expect to see annual year-over-year downtown condominium appreciation settle back to between 8% and 12% for 2018.

HERE'S THE FREE STUFF YOU CAN GET FROM US

Helping Toronto Home Buyers Achieve Their Goals Since 1980

As successful Toronto Realtors helping condo and house buyers and sellers since 1980, we've developed many programs and services to assist people with their real estate needs. Here are some of the plans of action we have designed to help.

Exclusively For Toronto Condo Or House SELLERS...

Sometimes people start thinking about selling their property years ahead of time and others jump right in and sell their condo or house within a few days or weeks.

Do you like to understand how something works before committing to it?

Either way, it makes sense to spend some time learning the right way to sell and avoiding making costly mistakes on one of the biggest sales of your life.

We've written a book to completely explain the best ways to get your condo sold for a higher price. And we've got special programs designed to help you achieve that.

If you are going to sell your home in the next 1 to 9 months, what you undertake right now can make a difference of thousands of dollars in your sale price, and there are some simple things you can do forthwith to make sure you get "Top-Dollar" when you do sell.

Insider Tips For Getting The Best Price - The Complete Guide To Selling Your Toronto Condo

By reading this book you're on your way to helping yourself have a successful sale and getting the highest price possible. As the saying goes 'Knowledge Is Power'. In this book, I will be telling you how my Team and I approach selling Toronto homes.

I've worked through three recessions since 1980 and now one of the longest stretches of market appreciation in Toronto's history.

So, I've seen it all... extreme buyer's markets and now extreme seller's markets... but in every instance, a competent, knowledgeable Realtor adds value to every seller when they're ready to enter the market.

Download the Book for free at **GettingTheBestPrice.ca**.

Timeline = 3-6 months before selling

A Quick Way To Find Out What Your Condo or House Could Be Worth In Today's Market

Before you start making any plans to move up, move down or move out to a rental, you'll need to know a market value price for what your home is worth in today's market.

The best way to do this is to have us complete a FREE "Pin-Point Price" Analysis, where I can take a closer in-person look at your condo and prepare a very specific price for your suite. This price will be more precise than the general range that you can get automatically from any website - and we guarantee in writing to sell your condo at the "Pin-Point Price" or higher in less than 32 days.

Go online to **PinPointPriceAnalysis.com** and fill in your property's specifics... it's that easy.

Timeline = 1-12 months before selling

Increase Your Home's Value With Simple Cosmetic Fix-Ups

So, you're happy with the price you could get... what's next?

The absolute best next step is for us to do a FREE "**Room-By-Room Review**", where I take a 20-minute walk-thru of your condominium and make specific recommendations about which fix-ups or improvements you should (and should not) do to prepare your suite for sale. I will point out the lowest cost, highest return improvements you can make to help sell your condo quickly and for more money.

Set up your Room-By-Room Review at **RoomByRoomReview.com**.

Timeline = 1-4 months before selling

Sell Your Condo In As Little As 24 Hours - And Laugh To Yourself At How Easy It Was

Some home owners are sensitive to having a lot of people traipsing through their home or there's some limitation as to their putting the condo on the public MLS system.

If that's you, one solution is to include your condo in our "**Silent Market**" of condominiums that are not yet on the open market.

Because we generate so much buyer interest from our website, Facebook and Google advertising and other proactive marketing, we may be able to find a buyer for your condo without even putting it on the market… saving you both time and money.

Register your condo 'silently' for sale at **SilentMarketForCondos.com**.

Timeline = 1-3 months before deciding to put your condo on the MLS system.

Exclusively For CONDO or HOUSE BUYERS…

It's often the same for buyers… sometimes they begin thinking about buying real estate years ahead and others plunge right in and purchase a new condo or house in just a few months.

It certainly is a wise idea to spend some time learning the right way to buy and avoiding making costly mistakes on one of the biggest purchases of their life.

Our **Home Buyer University** has created several ways for you to improve your knowledge about the home buying process and how Toronto's real estate market works right now.

Enroll in as many of these options as you'd like and be all set to go when the time is right for you. Under each option is a timeline of when ideally, you'd want to be taking advantage of these free services.

Perfect If You're 6-24 Months Away From Buying A Toronto Home

It always pays to get prepared. We've designed a Buyer University educational series with articles either bi-weekly or monthly designed to teach condo and house buyers about the home buying process in Toronto in a systematic way.

Go to **Home-Buyer-University.com** and complete the Buyer University registration.

Timeline = 6-24 months before purchasing

Create A Down Payment Even If You Have Nothing Saved Right Now

Would you like to buy your first Toronto condo or house but don't have a large, or any, down payment saved right now?

Our Free Government Money Report will show you how to grow or add to your down payment if you're a first-time home buyer.

Download it for free at **FreeGovernmentMoneyReport.com**.

Timeline = 6-24 months before purchasing

Home Buying Advice For 1st-Time Or Experienced Buyers

Do you like to understand how something works before committing to it?

The **Ultimate Toronto Home Buyer's Guide** will take you through the entire home buying process in a comprehensive way and help take away the stress of buying one of the most expensive purchases in your lifetime.

Download the Guide for free at **UltimateHomeBuyersGuide.com**.

Timeline = 3-18 months before purchasing

Get MLS Listings Sent To You Daily Just Like Realtors See

The customized **HOMEWatch Program** is perfect if you are several months away from seriously starting your home search.

Instead of randomly looking for homes on your own, you'll get information by email on all the new listings that come on the market in any price range and Toronto neighbourhood you choose.

Go to **CustomHomewatchSearch.com**.

Timeline = 3-12 months before purchasing

Beware Of Making Significant Home Buying Errors

Buying a home can be a confusing enterprise and many people don't know the best place to start. A **Starbucks Strategy Session** is a casual over-a-coffee conversation where you'll get your big and small questions answered to give you some terrific clarity about what to do next.

Remember, to achieve any goal you need a plan. The Starbucks Strategy Session is the best first step in setting up that plan.

Sign up at **StarbucksStrategySession.com**.

Timeline = 4-16 months before purchasing

Become A Competent Authority On Determining Value

When most folks are just starting to think about buying a condo or house, they typically don't have an accurate idea of what they can get for the money. They're often worried that they're too far away from the time they want to seriously start looking and don't want to bother an agent to see some homes just for the experience.

The **Market Experience Tour** is designed to help you get a feel for what's out there in the market in the neighbourhoods and price ranges that you feel comfortable with, without you having to worry about bringing your cheque book along.

This Tour is not designed to find your dream home… it provides an opportunity for you to get educated and find out what home styles, layouts and price ranges work best for you well before you're ready to seriously start your home search.

Market Experience Tours happen almost every day of the week… just pick the time, price range and neighbourhoods that suit your lifestyle.

When's the best time for you to check out some neighbourhoods? Choose at **MarketExperienceTour.com**.

Timeline = 4-16 months before purchasing

Avoid Costly Mistakes When Getting Pre-Approved For A Mortgage

Understanding what is involved in arranging the perfect mortgage for your lifestyle is critical when buying a condo or house.

The free **Home Buyer's Financing Guide eBook** will give you clear advice about how to arrange the right mortgage for you and your family. You'll gain the confidence you need when buying a Toronto home in today's busy seller's market.

You can download the book at **HomeBuyersFinancingGuide.com**.

Timeline = 4-12 months before purchasing

How Large A Mortgage Do You Qualify For?

Often people mistakenly think that going to an online site or having a quick, casual conversation with a bank rep to find out everything they need about getting a mortgage approval but this is absolutely not the case.

The perfect solution to getting a full mortgage pre-approval is to have a private, in-depth conversation with a mortgage professional who will review your personal financial situation and offer options about the best way to move forward.

A typical Mortgage Consultation takes about 20-30 minutes and you'll walk away with a mortgage pre-approval that you can feel confident about.

Set up that very important step at **FullMortgagePreApproval.com.**

Timeline = 3-9 months before purchasing

Here's A Simple Way To Save Time And Money When Starting Your Home Search

OK, so now you're ready to start seriously looking for your new home.

You've read up about how the home buying process works, you've been receiving some targeted listings from various Toronto neighbourhoods, you've been on a few (or several) Market Experience Tours to get a feel for the current market and your full mortgage pre-approval is in place.

The next big step is to meet up with your buyer agent for a comprehensive, in-office or online **Buyer Consultation** so you're fully prepared when you hit the bricks looking for that perfect condo or house.

A Buyer Consultation with an experienced, professional agent should take approximately 60 minutes… there's a lot to cover and understand and you don't want to make any mistakes or get stressed out in the process.

Go to **BuyerConsultation.com.**

Timeline = 3-5 months before purchasing

Here's How To Get In Touch...

Thomas Cook
Real Estate Sales Representative @ RE/MAX Hallmark Realty Ltd Brokerage

Mobile | 647-962-1650
Office | 416-465-7850

Web | Set up your own custom listings search at
www.Search.LivingInToronto.com

Email | Thomas@LivingInToronto.com

Experience || Thousands of homes sold since 1980
Professional Designations || ABR, SRES
Awards || RE/MAX's 2ND highest award - Circle Of Legends
Charity Support || Over $117,500 contributed to the Toronto Sick Kids Hospital
Speaker & Agent Coach || Delivered seminars and presentations to the public and Realtors about buying and selling real estate since 1995

www.ingramcontent.com/pod-product-compliance
Lightning Source LLC
Chambersburg PA
CBHW070157230526
45471CB00002B/708